END OF LIFE PLANNER

WHAT YOU WANT YOUR FAMILY TO KNOW WHEN YOU ARE GONE

WADE HOLLIS

Created with Vellum

CONTENTS

Introduction v

1. GETTING STARTED WITH PLANNING 1
   1.1 Why End-of-Life Planning Matters 1
   1.2 Overcoming Emotional Barriers 2
   1.3 Setting Clear Objectives for Your Planner 4
   1.4 How to Use This Planner Effectively 6
   1.5 Key Legal Documents You Need 8
   1.6 Creating a Timeline for Your Planning 10

2. ESSENTIAL LEGAL DOCUMENTATION 13
   2.1 Drafting a Will 13
   2.2 Preparing Your Living Will 19
   2.3 Understanding Power of Attorney 21
   2.4 Drafting Advance Directives 23
   2.5 Creating a Trust 25

3. FINANCIAL AFFAIRS AND ASSETS 28
   3.1 Inventory of Bank Accounts 28
   3.2 Documenting Investments and Stocks 30
   3.3 Managing Debts and Liabilities 32
   3.4 Insurance Policies and Coverage 34
   3.5 Real Estate and Property Documentation 36
   3.6 Handling Retirement Accounts 38

4. DIGITAL AND ONLINE PRESENCE 41
   4.1 Organizing Your Passwords 41
   4.2 Documenting Social Media Accounts 43
   4.3 Managing Email Accounts 45
   4.4 Handling Online Subscriptions and Services 47
   4.5 Digital Legacy Planning 49
   4.6 Tips for Securing Digital Information 51

Help Others Plan for the Future 55

5. MEDICAL INFORMATION AND HEALTH CARE 57
5.1 Recording Your Medical History 57
5.2 Documenting Current Medications 59
5.3 Contact Information for Healthcare Providers 62
5.4 Health Insurance Details 64
5.5 Planning for Long-Term Care 66

6. FUNERAL AND MEMORIAL WISHES 69
6.1 Choosing Burial or Cremation 69
6.2 Detailed Funeral Service Plans 72
6.3 Pre-Arranged Funeral Plans 74
6.4 Writing Your Obituary 76
6.5 Memorial Service Preferences 77
6.6 Selecting a Funeral Home 79

7. PERSONAL LETTERS AND MESSAGES 82
7.1 Writing Letters to Family Members 82
7.2 Crafting Messages for Friends 84
7.3 Creating a Video Message 86
7.4 Sharing Wisdom and Life Lessons 88
7.5 Personalizing Farewell Notes 90
7.6 Storing and Presenting Your Messages 92

8. FINAL DETAILS AND SPECIAL INSTRUCTIONS 94
8.1 Pet Care Instructions 94
8.2 Listing Emergency Contacts 96
8.3 Organizing Important Documents and Locations 98
8.4 Special Instructions for Personal Belongings 100
8.5 Regularly Updating Your Planner 102
8.6 Ensuring Accessibility and Security 103

Conclusion 107
Happiness Begins with Action 109
Bibliography 111

INTRODUCTION

A few years ago, I sat down with a woman, who we will call Mary, who was in her late seventies. Mary was scared—not of dying, but of leaving her family in chaos. She worried about the legal and financial mess she might leave behind. She feared her family may not know or be able to respect her final wishes. Together, we worked through her concerns, creating a detailed plan for her end-of-life care. The relief on her face was palpable. She told me she could finally sleep at night, knowing her family would be taken care of and her wishes honored.

This experience, among many others, propelled me to write this book. I have seen firsthand how end-of-life planning can bring peace of mind to seniors and their families. I aim to provide clear, easy-to-follow guidance on communicating your wishes to your loved ones. This book aims to cover everything you need—from legal documents to personal messages, from financial affairs to funeral arrangements.

Planning for the end of life is not just about you but also about your family. Studies show that families with clear end-of-life plans experience less stress and fewer conflicts. According to the National Institute on Aging, having a plan can prevent legal complications and ensure that your wishes are honored. Additionally, a survey conducted by the AARP found that 60% of adults believe it is essential to talk about end-of-life care, but only 56% have done so. This gap highlights the need for a structured approach to these difficult conversations.

My vision for this book is to guide you through every aspect of end-of-life planning. We will start with the basics, like creating a will and setting up a healthcare proxy. We'll move on to more personal elements, such as writing letters to loved ones and planning your funeral. The aim is to leave no stone unturned so you can rest easy knowing everything is taken care of.

This book is specifically for seniors thinking about their future and want to ensure their wishes are known and respected. You may have specific needs or concerns that we will address, such as dealing with chronic illness, managing family dynamics, or navigating legal complexities. Each chapter is designed to tackle these issues head-on, providing practical advice and actionable steps.

The structure of this book is straightforward. We will focus on legal and financial planning in the first few chapters. These sections will guide you through creating a will, setting up trusts, and understanding power of attorney. Next, we will delve into healthcare decisions, including advance directives and choosing a healthcare proxy. The latter chapters will cover personal aspects, such as writing letters and planning your funeral. Each chapter ends with a checklist to ensure you have covered all necessary steps.

As you embark on this journey with me, know you are taking a crucial step towards peace of mind. By the end of this book, you will have a detailed, user-friendly plan that comforts you and your loved ones. You will understand what needs to be done, why it is essential, and how to do it.

So, let's get started. Approach this journey with an open mind and a willingness to engage with each chapter. The steps you take now will bring you peace and help your family during one of the most challenging times of their lives. Your future, and theirs, will be all the brighter for it.

1
GETTING STARTED WITH PLANNING

1.1 WHY END-OF-LIFE PLANNING MATTERS

End-of-life planning offers significant emotional and practical benefits. When you know your affairs are in order, you gain peace of mind that cannot be overstated. This peace extends to your loved ones, who will face less stress and fewer uncertainties during a challenging time. Clear communication of your final wishes ensures your desires are respected, reducing the likelihood of family disputes. When everyone knows exactly what you want, it prevents misunderstandings and conflicts, preserving family harmony.

Failing to plan can lead to a host of complications. Without a will, your estate becomes subject to intestate succession laws, which vary by state. These laws often favor spouses and children but can leave out other important people in your life. The lack of a clear plan can result in unresolved estate issues and prolonged legal battles over asset distribution. Additionally, your family may face a financial burden as they navigate probate, court fees, and possible debts you left behind. For example, without a will, the court decides on asset distribution, often leading to prolonged and costly probate processes.

Contrary to common misconceptions, end-of-life planning is not only for the wealthy or those with complex estates. Everyone, regardless of financial status, needs to plan. Even if you have modest assets, your wishes for their distribution should be clear. Planning is also crucial for individuals without dependents. You might want to leave something to friends, charities, or other causes close to your heart. The absence of a plan can mean that your assets are distributed according to default state laws, which may not align with your desires.

In summary, end-of-life planning is essential for everyone. It provides peace of mind, reduces stress for loved ones, and ensures your wishes are respected. Addressing common misconceptions and illustrating the consequences of not planning can help us see the immense value of taking these steps.

It is about making informed decisions now to avoid complications later. Whether you have a vast estate or modest assets, whether you have dependents or not, end-of-life planning is crucial. By taking the time to plan, you ensure that your legacy is one of clarity and care rather than confusion and conflict.

1.2 OVERCOMING EMOTIONAL BARRIERS

Discussing end-of-life matters can be emotionally challenging. It's natural to feel a mix of fear and sadness when thinking about the end of life. These emotions are valid. Acknowledging this difficulty is the first step in overcoming it. Recognizing these feelings are common helps us understand that we are not alone in this journey. It is crucial to approach these conversations with empathy and understanding for yourself and your loved ones. The importance of empathy cannot be overstated; it allows us to connect on a deeper level and navigate these challenging discussions with compassion.

Managing emotional stress during this planning process requires practical strategies. Mindfulness exercises can be beneficial. Simple practices like deep breathing, meditation, or even a quiet walk can ground you and provide a sense of calm. These moments of mindfulness allow you to process your emotions in a healthy way. Journaling is another effective tool. Writing down your thoughts and feelings can provide clarity and relief. It helps you articulate your fears and hopes, making them more manageable. Professional counseling resources are also available for those who find the emotional weight too heavy to bear alone. Speaking with a therapist specializing in end-of-life issues can offer invaluable support and guidance.

Open communication with family members is another cornerstone of effective end-of-life planning. Starting the conversation can be the hardest part. One practical approach is to choose a quiet, private setting where everyone feels comfortable. Begin by expressing your feelings and emphasizing the importance of these discussions for everyone's peace of mind. For example, you might say, "I know this is a difficult topic, but I want to make sure my wishes are clear so that you all have less to worry about." Creating a comfortable environment for these talks can make a significant difference. Be patient and allow for emotional reactions. Some family members might initially resist or feel uncomfortable. Addressing this discomfort with empathy and reiterating the importance of the discussion can help ease their concerns.

Completing the planning process has profound positive outcomes. Many who have gone through it report a strong sense of relief and empowerment. This sense of accomplishment can also positively impact family dynamics. When everyone is on the same page, it fosters a sense of unity and shared understanding. Knowing that you have taken these steps can provide a lasting sense of peace and fulfillment.

Overcoming emotional barriers is a critical aspect of end-of-life planning. Recognizing the difficulty, employing coping strategies, fostering open communication, and focusing on positive outcomes can transform this challenging process into a meaningful and empowering experience. This chapter aims to equip you with the tools and understanding needed to navigate these emotional waters, ensuring that your final wishes bring peace and clarity to you and your loved ones.

1.3 SETTING CLEAR OBJECTIVES FOR YOUR PLANNER

When creating an end-of-life planner, the first step is to define your goals. What do you hope to accomplish through this process? One of the primary objectives should be ensuring legal preparedness. This means having all necessary legal documents, such as a will, power of attorney, and advance directives. These documents protect your wishes and provide clear guidance to your loved ones during a difficult time. Legal preparedness eliminates ambiguity and ensures your decisions are honored, preventing potential conflicts and legal disputes.

Equally important is documenting financial information. This includes detailing your bank accounts, investments, insurance policies, and other assets. Clearly outlining your financial situation provides a roadmap for your family to follow. This helps them manage your estate and meet any outstanding obligations. Financial documentation can also include instructions for accessing digital assets, like online banking and investment accounts. The aim is to make the financial transition as smooth as possible for your loved ones.

Another crucial goal is communicating your medical wishes. Advance directives, living wills, and healthcare proxies are tools that ensure your medical preferences are known and respected. These documents guide your family and healthcare providers in making decisions that align with your values and desires. Whether you have specific treatments you want or wish to avoid, documenting these preferences can alleviate the burden on your loved ones, who might otherwise struggle to make these decisions on your behalf.

Once you've defined your goals, it's essential to prioritize critical areas. Start by identifying which sections of the planner are most important to you. Financial documentation is often a significant concern, as it involves many details and can have substantial implications for your estate. Begin by gathering statements, account numbers, and contact information for your financial institutions. This information will serve as the foundation for your financial section.

Next, focus on medical directives. These documents should be comprehensive and precise, covering various scenarios. Take the time to discuss your medical wishes with your healthcare providers and loved ones. Ensure that everyone understands your preferences and that the documents are easily accessible in an emergency. Medical directives are not just about end-of-life care; they also cover situations where you might be temporarily incapacitated and unable to communicate your wishes.

Funeral arrangements are another critical area to address. Planning your funeral can relieve your family of the stress and uncertainty that often accompanies such events. Decide whether you prefer burial or cremation, and specify any particular services or rituals you want. Documenting these details ensures that your final farewell aligns with your values and beliefs.

Establishing a realistic timeline for completing different sections of the planner is essential. Setting achievable milestones helps you stay organized and motivated. Start with short-term goals, such as gathering financial information and initial family discussions. These tasks are often straightforward and can be completed relatively quickly. As you progress, set long-term goals that require more time and effort, like creating a trust fund or finalizing medical directives. Breaking down the process into manageable steps prevents it from becoming overwhelming and allows you to make steady progress.

This book provides examples and templates to assist you in setting clear objectives. For instance, a completed financial section might include a list of bank accounts, account numbers, and contact information for financial advisors. A template for documenting medical history can guide you in recording essential details like past surgeries, chronic conditions, and current medications. A sample timeline can also help you structure your planning process, outlining short-term and long-term goals with specific deadlines.

By defining your goals, prioritizing key areas, and establishing a realistic timeline, you create a clear roadmap for your end-of-life planning. This structured approach ensures that no aspect is overlooked and that each step is completed thoroughly. With the help of examples and templates, you can confidently navigate the planning process, knowing that you are taking meaningful steps to protect your wishes and support your loved ones.

1.4 HOW TO USE THIS PLANNER EFFECTIVELY

Understanding the layout of your planner is crucial to making the most of it. The planner is divided into several sections, each dedicated to a specific aspect of end-of-life planning. These sections are clearly labeled with tabs for easy navigation. You'll find sections for legal documents, financial affairs, medical directives, personal messages, and funeral arrangements. Each tab guides you to a comprehensive part of the planner, making locating the information you need simple. Additionally, the planner includes a table of contents at the beginning, offering an overview of what each section entails. This structure ensures you can quickly find and update any part of your plan without feeling overwhelmed.

Filling out each section requires a systematic approach. Start with the legal documents section. Here, you will find step-by-step guides for completing essential documents like your will, power of attorney, and advance directives. Each guide includes a checklist to ensure you gather all necessary information before you begin. For example, when filling out your will, the checklist will remind you to list all your assets, identify your beneficiaries, and designate an executor. The medical directives section provides similar guidance, helping you document your healthcare preferences and appoint a medical proxy. Following these step-by-step instructions ensures that no detail is overlooked and your documents are sound. However, always consult a lawyer licensed in your state to help ensure your documents are legally enforceable.

Interactive elements are a crucial feature of this planner, designed to engage you actively in the planning process. Each section includes checklists and prompts to guide your thinking and ensure you cover all necessary aspects. For instance, the financial affairs section includes prompts for listing all your bank accounts, investments, and insurance policies. Spaces for personal notes and letters allow you to add a personal touch, making your planner uniquely yours. Additionally, some sections include QR codes that link to online resources for further information. These resources include legal templates, financial planning tools, or medical directive forms. Engaging with these interactive elements makes the planning process more comprehensive and personalized.

Regular updates to your planner are essential for keeping it accurate and relevant. Life is dynamic, and your circumstances can change. An annual review of your planner ensures that all information remains current. Set aside a specific time each year to revisit and update each section. Major life events, such as the birth of a grandchild, the sale of a property, or changes in your health, also necessitate updates. Addressing these changes promptly is crucial to ensure your planner always reflects your current wishes and situation. Keeping the planner secure yet accessible is another essential consideration. Store it in a safe place, such as a locked drawer or a fireproof safe, but ensure your trusted family members know where to find it and how to access it.

By understanding the layout, using the step-by-step guides, engaging with the interactive elements, and regularly updating your planner, you ensure that your end-of-life planning is thorough and effective. This planner is more than just a collection of forms; it is a tool designed to bring clarity and peace of mind. Each section, from legal documents to personal messages, has been crafted to guide you through the planning process in a straightforward, manageable way. Engaging with each part of the planner, following the structured guides, and keeping everything updated ensures that your final wishes are clear and that your loved ones are spared unnecessary stress and confusion.

1.5 KEY LEGAL DOCUMENTS YOU NEED

Identifying and understanding the key legal documents required for end-of-life planning is vital. These documents ensure your wishes are respected and provide clear guidance for your loved ones. The first crucial document is a **will**. A will is a legal document that describes how you would like your assets to be distributed after your death. It also can address issues like guardianship for children, dependents, and pets. The next is a **living will**. This outlines your medical treatment preferences if you cannot communicate them yourself. It details the types of medical care you do or do not want, such as life support or resuscitation efforts. The living will becomes your voice when you cannot speak, ensuring your healthcare preferences are followed.

Another essential document is the **power of attorney**. This legal instrument allows you to appoint someone you trust to make financial and legal decisions on your behalf if you become incapacitated. Different types of power of attorney exist, including general, durable, and medical. The durable power of attorney remains in effect if you become incapacitated, whereas the general power of attorney does not. The medical power of attorney, also known as a healthcare proxy, specifically grants authority to make medical decisions. Selecting the right person for this role is critical, as they will have significant control over your affairs.

Advance directives encompass both the living will and the medical power of attorney. These directives provide comprehensive instructions for your healthcare preferences and designate a medical decision-maker. Having advance directives in place ensures that your medical care aligns with your values and wishes, even when you cannot communicate them. These documents also alleviate the burden on your family, who might otherwise struggle to make these decisions without knowing your preferences.

The importance of these documents cannot be overstated. They offer legal protection for your wishes, ensuring your decisions are honored. By clearly outlining your preferences, you simplify the decision-making process for your family, reducing their emotional and practical burden. These documents also help avoid legal disputes that can arise without explicit instructions. For example, without a living will, family members might disagree on the appropriate medical care, leading to conflicts and prolonged legal battles. Having these documents in place provides clarity and prevents such disputes.

Completing these documents requires attention to detail. Begin with templates and examples that provide a structured format for your information. Many states offer free advance directive forms online, which can be a helpful starting point. When filling out a living will, be specific about your preferences. For instance, if you do not want to be kept on life support if there is no reasonable chance of recovery, clearly state this. Ensure your power of attorney document includes all necessary details, such as the scope of authority and any limitations.

To ensure legal validity, follow your state's requirements for notarization and witnessing. This step is crucial for making the documents legally binding. Make sure to keep copies of these documents in a safe but accessible place. Inform your designated agents and family members where they can find these documents in case of an emergency.

If you need additional help, several resources are available. Legal aid organizations can assist at little to no cost. They often offer workshops and consultations to help you complete these documents correctly. Online legal resources, such as LegalZoom, Rocket Lawyer, and Nolo, provide templates and step-by-step guides. These platforms can simplify the process and ensure you meet all legal requirements. Hiring a professional attorney is viable for those who prefer personalized assistance. An attorney can offer tailored advice and ensure your documents are comprehensive and legally sound.

You take proactive steps to protect your wishes and support your loved ones by identifying and completing these vital legal documents. Each document serves a specific purpose, collectively ensuring that your end-of-life care and affairs are managed according to your preferences. The peace of mind that comes with knowing your decisions will be respected is invaluable, making this effort well worth the time and care it requires.

1.6 CREATING A TIMELINE FOR YOUR PLANNING

Establishing a clear timeline for your end-of-life planning can make the process far more manageable. Setting short-term goals is a practical way to get started and build momentum. Begin by gathering all personal information, such as birth certificates, marriage licenses, and Social Security numbers. These documents form the foundation of your plan and are essential for completing other sections. Initial family discussions are another critical short-term goal. These conversations may feel daunting, but they are necessary for ensuring everyone is on the same page. Start by sharing your intentions and explaining the importance of planning. This openness will lay the groundwork for more detailed discussions later.

After these initial steps, focus on starting with essential legal documents. This includes drafting a simple will, setting up a power of attorney, and creating advance directives. These documents are the backbone of any end-of-life plan and provide a legal framework for your wishes. Completing these tasks early on can give you a sense of accomplishment and provide immediate protection for your decisions. Breaking down these tasks into smaller, manageable steps can make the process less overwhelming and more achievable.

Once you have tackled your short-term goals, it's time to set long-term objectives. These more complex tasks will take additional time and effort to complete. One of the most important long-term goals is completing your financial documentation. This involves detailing all your assets, liabilities, and financial accounts. Include information about investments, retirement accounts, and insurance policies. This comprehensive financial overview will be invaluable to your family when managing your estate. Another critical objective is finalizing your medical directives. These documents should be detailed and cover various scenarios to ensure your healthcare wishes are respected. Discuss these directives with your healthcare providers and update them as needed.

Planning your funeral arrangements is another significant long-term goal. Deciding on burial or cremation, selecting a funeral home, and outlining the details of your service are all essential steps. Documenting these preferences will relieve your family of making these decisions during an emotionally charged time. Consider writing a personal message or letter to be read at your service, adding a meaningful touch to your farewell. These long-term objectives require careful thought and planning but are crucial for fully realizing your wishes.

Regular check-ins are essential to keep your plan current and effective. Schedule quarterly reviews to revisit each section and make any necessary updates. Life changes, such as the birth of a grandchild or the sale of a property, can impact your plan, and it's essential to address these changes promptly. Annual updates are also recommended to ensure all information remains accurate and relevant. This might include updating financial documents, revising medical directives, or adding new personal messages. Regularly reviewing and updating your plan ensures it remains a true reflection of your wishes.

Flexibility is vital in your timeline to accommodate life changes and unforeseen circumstances. Adjust your goals as needed to reflect your current situation. Allow yourself time for emotional processing, especially when dealing with sensitive tasks such as writing personal messages or planning your funeral. Taking breaks and revisiting these tasks when you feel ready is okay. Seeking help when necessary is also essential. Whether consulting with a legal professional, discussing your medical directives with a healthcare provider, or seeking emotional support from a counselor, don't hesitate to ask for assistance. Flexibility ensures that your plan remains relevant and manageable, regardless of what life throws your way.

Creating a timeline for your end-of-life planning involves:

- Setting short-term goals to get started.
- Establishing long-term objectives for more complex tasks.
- Scheduling regular check-ins to keep your plan current.
- Incorporating flexibility to adapt to life changes.

This structured approach ensures that each aspect of your plan is addressed thoroughly and thoughtfully. By taking these steps, you can achieve a comprehensive and effective end-of-life plan that brings peace of mind to you and your loved ones.

2
ESSENTIAL LEGAL DOCUMENTATION

This chapter aims to guide you through preparing the essential legal documents including a will and advanced directives, ensuring that your medical preferences are clearly documented and legally binding.

2.1 DRAFTING A WILL

Whether your estate is large or small, your estate has to pass through a process called probate when you pass away. A will is like a set of instructions that your loved ones and the court will use to dispose of your assets in accordance with your wishes. Without one, default rules decide who gets what without your input.

There are ten essential steps to making your will:

1. Decide how you want to draft your will.
2. List the assets to distribute through your will.
3. Choose the beneficiaries who will receive your assets.
4. Choose and name your executor.
5. Select a guardian for your children.

6. Leave any gifts to charities.
7. Sign your will in front of witnesses, following the formal requirements in your state.
8. Store your will in a safe place.
9. Tell your executor and loved ones about your plans and the location of your will.
10. Review your will and update regularly.

First, choose how you want to draft a will. There are several ways; you can do it yourself, using an online tool like FreeWill or purchase forms or templates from companies like LegalZoom, Rocket Lawyer, or Nolo. You can also hire a lawyer to do all or part of the drafting. To prepare for drafting your will, whether entirely on your own or with the help of a professional, create a list of:

- all your assets, including physical property like your home, furnishings, your vehicles such as cars and boats, and other real estate;
- financial assets like bank accounts, money market accounts, certificates of deposit, stocks, bonds, and cryptocurrency;
- pets – they feel like family, but the law treats them as property, so be sure to consider who would make a good caretaker for them;
- family heirlooms and valuable personal property, like jewelry, firearms, and china.

Start by creating a comprehensive list of everything you own, in whole or in part. Some assets, however, are called "non-probate" assets because they pass to your beneficiaries directly rather than through a will. Some of those assets include:

- Assets in a trust. Trusts are discussed below, but essentially, assets placed in a trust are transferred to your named beneficiaries based on the terms of the trust documents rather than your will.

- Life insurance. These policies require you to name a beneficiary paid on your policy per the insurance contract.
- Retirement accounts. 401(k) accounts are paid directly to your named beneficiaries like life insurance.
- POD (Payable on Death) or TOD (Transfer on Death) accounts are bank accounts that allow you to designate a beneficiary, similar to how you do with life insurance and retirement accounts.
- Stocks or bonds with a beneficiary. Some investment assets may allow you to name a beneficiary paid directly outside your will.
- Any jointly owned property. Your portion of jointly owned property can pass through your will, but some property owned partly by a partner or spouse transfers automatically upon death. Check your local laws.

Next, decide who you want to receive your assets. Name them clearly in your will. Use this opportunity to check and update who you have named as a beneficiary on your non-probate assets and to choose who you want to name in your will.

Next, you must choose an executor. Selecting an executor is one of the most critical decisions in your end-of-life planning. The executor's role is multifaceted, involving the management of your estate, ensuring your wishes are carried out, and handling various legal and financial matters. This person will be responsible for gathering your assets, paying debts or taxes, and distributing the remaining estate according to your will. They must navigate complex legal processes, which often include probate court. The executor's role is crucial in maintaining order and adhering to your final wishes, making it essential to choose someone reliable and competent.

When selecting the right person for this critical role, consider both their qualities and their relationship to you. Look for someone who is organized, trustworthy, and has good judgment. They should be capable of handling financial matters and navigating legal requirements. Potential candidates often include family members, close friends, or professionals like attorneys or accountants. Discussing the role with your potential executor is vital to ensure they understand and are willing to take on these responsibilities. This conversation can also help clarify any questions and ensure they are prepared for the task ahead. Remember, the person you choose will play a significant role in managing your affairs after you're gone, so selecting someone who can handle the responsibility with care and efficiency is crucial.

Legally appointing an executor involves several steps. First, you must include the designation in your will. Clearly state the name of your chosen executor and any alternates in case your primary choice is unable or unwilling to serve. Next, you must follow the required documentation processes, which typically involve signing your will in the presence of witnesses. The specific requirements can vary by state, so it's essential to ensure that you meet all legal criteria. Proper documentation and adherence to legal requirements are crucial for the smooth execution of your wishes.

Supporting your executor in their role is essential to make their job easier and ensure your estate is managed effectively. Begin by providing clear instructions in your will, detailing how you want your assets to be managed and distributed. Organize all necessary documents, such as financial records, property deeds, and insurance policies, in an easy-to-access and understandable way. Regularly update these documents to reflect any changes in your estate or personal wishes. Keeping your executor informed of these updates helps them stay prepared and reduces the likelihood of confusion or errors. Additionally, consider creating a contact list of key individuals and institutions your executor might need to contact, such as financial advisors, attorneys, and family members.

When choosing an executor, it's also essential to consider the potential emotional toll on the person you select. Managing an estate can be a time-consuming and emotionally challenging task, particularly if the executor is also grieving your loss. Discussing the role candidly with your chosen executor can help them understand the scope of their responsibilities and prepare them mentally for the task. Providing them with resources and support, such as the contact information of legal and financial professionals, can also make the process less overwhelming.

If you have minor children, you should choose a guardian for them in your will. Your child's other parent will usually become the sole custodian and guardian when you pass. However, if both parents die at the same time or the other parent predeceases you or is unable to care for the children, the court system will have to determine who will have custody of your children. If there are no volunteers to take custody of your children, they may become wards of the state and enter the foster care system.

Being a guardian is an enormous responsibility. Make sure your nominated guardian is willing to raise your children. Naturally, this should be someone you trust deeply with your children and their future. Like an executor, you can name a backup guardian if your first cannot fulfill their role. Some people set aside money for their appointed guardians to help offset the financial cost.

Next, consider whether you want to leave anything to charitable organizations. You may include nonprofit organizations as beneficiaries in your will. You may choose to leave money or property to charity. It would be best if you were sure to include the charitable organization's full name, address, and Employer Identification Number (EIN).

You must next ensure your will meets your state's formal requirements. You must sign it in your own handwriting, and most states require that you sign in front of two witnesses, who will also sign your will. Witnesses should be legal adults (18 in most states) and of sound mind. Your witnesses shouldn't be anyone listed in your will, whether an executor, guardian, or any beneficiary such as children or other family members.

At the time of this writing, Louisiana is the only state that requires a will to be notarized to be valid. However, you may want to create something known as a self-proving affidavit. This involves having a notarized document that proves your will, making it easier to prove your will and streamline the process of distributing your estate. They are options and not recognized in every state. Consult a lawyer licensed in your state to ensure your will complies with the formal requirements of your state.

Next, store your will in a safe place like a fireproof safe or an attorney's office. Consider making a scanned copy of the will and placing it in a digital vault. Also, consider storing other important estate planning documents in the same place as your will, such as titles, deeds, life insurance policies, online password information, and any other documents collected as part of this planning process. Tell your executor and loved ones where they can find your will and other essential documents. This will make it easier for your executor to find all your important documents after you pass.

Finally, update your will regularly. Update it every three to five years and every time you have a significant life event, such as:

- Marriage or divorce.
- Having children or grandchildren.
- Moving to a new state.
- Death of a beneficiary, executor, guardian, or other significant person.

Consider setting a digital calendar reminder to look at these documents. Perhaps tax time would be a good time because financial issues are often already on your mind.

2.2 PREPARING YOUR LIVING WILL

A living will is a legal document that outlines your medical wishes if you cannot communicate them yourself. It is essential to end-of-life planning, ensuring your autonomy is protected in medical decisions. The living will specifies the types of medical treatments you want or do not want, providing clear instructions to healthcare providers and loved ones. This document becomes your voice when you cannot speak, ensuring your healthcare preferences are honored.

Creating a living will involves several steps. First, you need to identify your medical treatment preferences. This requires you to reflect on your values and consider various medical scenarios. For instance, you may want to receive life-sustaining treatments such as mechanical ventilation or feeding tubes. It's essential to think about different situations, such as being in a persistent vegetative state or having a terminal illness. Specifying your preferences ensures that your medical care aligns with your values and desires.

Next, you need to specify your end-of-life care wishes. This includes decisions about pain management, organ donation, and any specific instructions for your care. For example, you might state that you want to receive palliative care to manage pain and improve your quality of life. Additionally, you can include personal preferences, such as wanting to be at home rather than in a hospital during your final days. These details provide clear guidance to your healthcare providers and loved ones, ensuring that your end-of-life care is tailored to your wishes.

Another important step is choosing a healthcare proxy. This is the person you trust to make medical decisions on your behalf if you cannot do so. Selecting someone who understands your values and is willing to advocate for your wishes is crucial. Discuss your preferences with your chosen proxy, ensuring they are comfortable with the responsibility. Documenting this appointment in your living will provides legal authority for your proxy to act on your behalf, giving you peace of mind that your wishes will be respected.

Legal requirements for a living will vary by state, so it is essential to ensure that your document meets the necessary criteria. Most states require that the living will be signed in the presence of witnesses and notarized to be legally binding. This step ensures that healthcare providers and legal authorities recognize the document. It's also a good idea to use state-specific forms, which can be found online or obtained from legal aid organizations. Completing these forms according to your state's regulations ensures that your living will is valid and enforceable.

Updating and storing your living will is an ongoing process. Regular reviews and updates are essential to ensure the document remains current and reflects any changes in your preferences or circumstances. For example, if you are diagnosed with a new medical condition or your treatment preferences change, you must update your living will accordingly. Safe storage options include keeping the document in a fireproof safe or with your attorney. It is also essential to inform your healthcare providers and family members about the existence and location of your living will. Providing copies to your primary care physician and your healthcare proxy ensures that the document is readily accessible when needed.

By preparing a living will, you take proactive steps to ensure that your medical wishes are respected and your autonomy is protected. This document provides clear guidance to your healthcare providers and loved ones, reducing the burden of decision-making during difficult times. Following the steps outlined in this chapter, you can create a living will that reflects your values and ensures that your end-of-life care aligns with your preferences.

Checklist for Preparing Your Living Will

- Identify your medical treatment preferences.
- Specify your end-of-life care wishes.
- Choose a trustworthy healthcare proxy.
- Ensure your living will meets state-specific legal requirements.

- Sign and notarize the document.
- Regularly review and update your living will.
- Store the document in a safe place.
- Inform healthcare providers and family members about the document's location.
- Provide copies to your primary care physician and healthcare proxy.

2.3 UNDERSTANDING POWER OF ATTORNEY

A power of attorney (POA) is a vital document that grants someone the authority to act on your behalf in legal, financial, or medical matters, depending on the type you choose. There are several forms of POA, each serving a specific purpose. The general power of attorney gives your appointed agent broad authority over your affairs. This can include managing your finances, signing documents, and making decisions you would typically handle yourself. It's helpful when you are temporarily unavailable or incapacitated but not permanently.

A durable power of attorney, however, continues to be effective even if you become incapacitated. This form of POA is essential for long-term planning, as it ensures that your agent can manage your affairs without interruption if you cannot make decisions yourself. The medical power of attorney, also known as a healthcare proxy, specifically grants authority to make medical decisions on your behalf. This is crucial for ensuring your healthcare preferences are respected when you cannot communicate them yourself. Each type of POA serves a unique role, and understanding these differences helps you choose the right one for your needs.

Choosing the right agent to act on your behalf is a critical decision. You need to select someone trustworthy and capable. Look for reliability, good judgment, and a clear understanding of your wishes. It's essential to have open and honest conversations with your potential agent to ensure they are comfortable with the responsibility and understand your expectations. Clear communication helps prevent misunderstandings and ensures your agent is prepared to act in your best interests. Be mindful of potential conflicts of interest. For instance, appointing someone who stands to benefit from your estate might lead to biased decisions. Selecting an impartial and objective agent can help mitigate these risks.

The legal process for establishing a power of attorney involves several steps. You'll need to complete the necessary forms, which vary by state but generally require detailed information about you, your agent, and the specific powers you are granting. Understanding the legal terminology and implications of each type of POA is essential. For example, specifying whether your POA is durable or limited to specific actions can have significant consequences. Once the forms are completed, they must typically be signed in the presence of witnesses and notarized to be legally binding. This ensures legal authorities and institutions recognize the document.

Over time, you may need to revoke or amend your power of attorney. Circumstances change, and your choice of agent or the powers granted might no longer be suitable. You can revoke a POA at any time, provided you are mentally competent. To do so, you must notify your agent in writing and retrieve any copies of the POA document. Legal amendment procedures involve creating a new POA that outlines the changes or completely revokes the previous document. Communicating these changes to all relevant parties, including financial institutions and healthcare providers, is crucial to ensure that the new POA is recognized and the old one is nullified.

Case Study: Choosing the Right Agent

Consider the story of Robert, who initially appointed his eldest son as his agent under a general power of attorney. Over time, he noticed that his son was struggling with his financial issues, which created a potential conflict of interest. Robert revoked the original POA and appointed his long-time friend, a retired accountant, as his new agent. This change ensured that his financial affairs were managed impartially, reflecting Robert's best interests without conflicts. This example underscores the importance of carefully choosing and, when necessary, re-evaluating your choice of agent to ensure your wishes are always honored.

Understanding the various forms of power of attorney and selecting the right agent involves careful consideration and legal steps. Each type of POA serves a specific purpose, from managing your finances to making medical decisions. Choosing a trustworthy and capable agent ensures that your affairs are handled according to your wishes. The legal process requires completing and notarizing the appropriate forms, and you must be prepared to revoke or amend the POA as circumstances change. By taking these steps, you ensure that your interests are protected and your decisions are respected, providing peace of mind for you and your loved ones.

2.4 DRAFTING ADVANCE DIRECTIVES

Drafting advance directives is one of the most pivotal steps in ensuring your medical wishes are honored. These legal documents serve as a clear guide for your healthcare providers and family members, outlining your medical treatment preferences if you cannot communicate them yourself. By documenting your wishes, you reduce the burden on your loved ones, who might otherwise be left to make difficult decisions without knowing your preferences. This clarity can prevent disputes and provide peace of mind, knowing that your medical care will align with your values.

Advance directives have several critical parts, each serving a unique function. One of the primary components is the living will, a document specifying the types of medical treatments you want or do not want. For instance, you might indicate whether you wish to receive life-sustaining treatments like mechanical ventilation or feeding tubes in certain conditions, such as being in a persistent vegetative state. The living will provide explicit instructions, ensuring your medical care aligns with your values and wishes.

Another essential part of advance directives is appointing a healthcare proxy. This person, also known as a durable power of attorney for healthcare, is entrusted to make medical decisions on your behalf if you cannot. Choosing someone who understands your values and is willing to advocate for your wishes is crucial. Discuss your preferences with your chosen proxy to ensure they are comfortable with the responsibility and fully aware of your desires. This appointment provides legal authority for your proxy to act on your behalf, giving you peace of mind that your medical preferences will be respected.

Do Not Resuscitate (DNR) orders are another component that can be included in your advance directives. A DNR order indicates that you do not want cardiopulmonary resuscitation (CPR) if your heart stops beating. This decision can be crucial for those with terminal illnesses or severe health conditions where resuscitation might prolong suffering without improving quality of life. Including a DNR order ensures that medical personnel clearly and legally recognize your wishes regarding resuscitation.

To make your advance directives legally binding, you must adhere to state-specific laws and regulations. Each state has its requirements, but generally, the documents need to be signed in the presence of witnesses and notarized. This process ensures the validity of the directives and their acceptance by healthcare providers. Using state-specific forms, which can often be found online or obtained from legal aid organizations, helps ensure that your advance directives meet all necessary criteria. Completing these forms accurately and following the legal steps makes your directives enforceable and respected.

Communicating your advance directives is as essential as drafting them. You must share copies with your family members, healthcare proxy, and primary care physician. This ensures everyone in your care knows your wishes and can act accordingly. Storing copies in accessible locations, such as a fireproof safe or with your attorney, makes it easier to retrieve them when needed. Additionally, including your advance directives in your medical records ensures they are readily available to healthcare providers during emergencies or routine care. Clear communication and easy access to these documents are crucial for effective implementation.

Resource List: Where to Find Advance Directive Forms

- State Health Departments: Many states provide free advance directive forms on their official health department websites.
- AARP: Offers forms and resources for advance care planning.
- American Bar Association: Provides guidance and templates for advance directives.
- National Hospice and Palliative Care Organization: Offers comprehensive resources for end-of-life planning.
- Online Platforms: Websites like PREPARE for Your Care and The Conversation Project offer tools and forms for drafting advance directives.

Advance directives are crucial in ensuring your medical wishes are honored and reducing the burden on your family. By clearly outlining your preferences, appointing a healthcare proxy, and including DNR orders, you provide explicit instructions for your care. Adhering to state-specific legal requirements and effectively communicating your directives ensures they are legally binding and respected by healthcare providers. Taking these steps protects your autonomy and provides peace of mind for you and your loved ones.

2.5 CREATING A TRUST

A trust is a legal entity that holds and manages assets on behalf of beneficiaries. There are various types of trusts, each serving different purposes. A revocable trust, for instance, allows you to retain control over the assets during your lifetime, enabling you to make changes or dissolve the trust as needed. In contrast, an irrevocable trust transfers control to a trustee, making it difficult to alter once established. The primary benefit of creating a trust is that it can help manage your assets during your lifetime and distribute them efficiently after your death, often bypassing the lengthy and costly probate process. Trusts can also offer tax advantages and provide a structured way to support beneficiaries who may need to be more capable of managing large sums of money independently.

The first step in establishing a trust fund is choosing the type of trust that best suits your needs. If you want flexibility, a revocable trust might be the best option. As the name implies, it is a trust that can be revoked during your life. This type of trust allows you to make changes as your circumstances evolve, enabling you to avoid the hassle and expense of a probate proceeding. However, an irrevocable trust might be more appropriate if you aim to protect assets from creditors or reduce estate taxes. The benefits and implications of the type of trust you choose are varied. Debtor-creditor laws can be complex. Tax law is undoubtedly complicated. These issues are beyond the scope of this short planner. You should consult licensed professionals in your state, such as lawyers and accountants, to discuss what kind of trust is best for your situation.

Once you've decided on the type of trust, the next step is selecting a trustee. This individual or institution will manage the trust's assets according to your terms. When choosing a trustee, look for someone trustworthy, financially savvy, and capable of managing the responsibilities. You can also opt for a professional trustee, such as a bank or a trust company, offering expertise and impartiality.

Funding the trust involves transferring assets into the trust's ownership. This can include real estate, bank accounts, investments, and other valuable items. To transfer real estate, you must execute a new deed that names the trust as the owner. You'll need to update the account titles for bank accounts and investments to reflect the trust's ownership. Keeping detailed records of all assets transferred into the trust is essential. This documentation ensures that the assets are properly managed and can be easily accounted for when it's time to distribute them to the beneficiaries.

Additionally, specific legal requirements and documentation are necessary to establish a trust. These often include a trust agreement, which outlines the terms and conditions of the trust, the trustee's responsibilities, and the beneficiaries' rights. The trustee has a fiduciary duty to act in the best interests of the beneficiaries, managing the assets prudently and distributing them according to the trust's terms.

Maintaining and updating the trust is an ongoing responsibility. Regular reviews ensure the trust remains aligned with your current wishes and financial situation. Life events such as marriage, divorce, the birth of a child, or the acquisition of new assets may necessitate updates to the trust. Keeping the trust current helps to prevent disputes and ensures that your assets are distributed according to your most recent intentions. Communicating with the trustee is also vital. Regular updates and clear instructions can help the trustee manage the assets effectively and address any issues promptly.

Creating a trust fund involves:

- Choosing the correct type of trust.
- Selecting a reliable trustee.
- Funding the trust with your assets.
- Understanding the legal and financial intricacies involved.

Regularly maintaining and updating the trust ensures that it continues to serve its intended purpose, providing peace of mind for you and your beneficiaries.

3
FINANCIAL AFFAIRS AND ASSETS

This chapter aims to guide you through documenting and organizing your financial affairs to ensure your peace of mind and that of your loved ones.

3.1 INVENTORY OF BANK ACCOUNTS

Start by listing all your checking and savings accounts. This involves documenting each account, including the bank name and branch. Note the type of account—whether a checking, savings, or money market account. It's essential to include the account numbers for each. This information will provide a clear overview of where your funds are held and make it easier for your loved ones to access these assets when needed. For instance, if you have a checking account at First National Bank and a savings account at Community Credit Union, list each separately with all relevant details.

Including online banking information is equally important. In today's digital age, many of us manage our finances online, and access to these accounts can be crucial. Document your online banking usernames and passwords. Additionally, include any security questions and answers associated with these accounts. This information ensures your loved ones can access your online accounts without unnecessary delays or complications. For example, if you use an online banking portal with a specific username and have security questions about your first pet's name or your mother's maiden name, write these down clearly. Instructions for accessing online accounts, such as the website URL or any special login procedures, should also be included.

Documenting account balances and statements is another critical step. Start by recording the current balance of each account. This information provides a snapshot of your financial standing. Monthly statements offer an ongoing record of transactions and balances, while year-end summaries comprehensively summarize your financial activity over the past year. Collect these statements and organize them in a dedicated folder or digital file. This practice helps manage your finances and simplifies the task for those handling your estate. For example, if your checking account has a balance of $5,000 and your savings account holds $10,000, note these amounts and keep the latest statements handy.

It's important to highlight the differences between joint and individual accounts. Joint accounts are those you share with a spouse or family member, allowing both parties access to the funds. Personal accounts, on the other hand, are solely in your name. Noting the ownership of each account is crucial, as it affects how the funds will be accessed and distributed. For instance, a joint account with your spouse will likely automatically transfer to them upon passing, whereas an individual account must go through probate. This distinction simplifies the process for your loved ones and ensures your assets are managed according to your wishes.

Checklist: Inventory of Bank Accounts

- List all checking and savings accounts.
- Bank name and branch
- Account numbers

- Types of accounts (checking, savings, money market)
- Include online banking information.
- Online banking usernames
- Passwords and security questions
- Instructions for accessing online accounts
- Document account balances and statements.
- Current balances
- Monthly statements
- Year-end summaries
- Highlight joint and individual accounts.
- Joint accounts with spouse or family members
- Individual accounts

Taking the time to detail these elements ensures that your financial affairs are transparent and accessible. This preparation not only eases the burden on your loved ones but also gives you confidence that your financial legacy will be managed according to your wishes.

3.2 DOCUMENTING INVESTMENTS AND STOCKS

Keeping track of your investments and stocks is crucial for managing your financial affairs effectively. Start by listing all your investment accounts in detail. This includes noting down the names of the brokerage firms where your accounts are held. For example, you might have accounts at firms like Fidelity, Charles Schwab, or Vanguard. Each account will have a unique number, which you should document carefully. Specify your investments in these accounts, such as stocks, bonds, and mutual funds. This level of detail helps create a clear picture of your investment portfolio, making it easier for your loved ones to manage these assets when the time comes.

When it comes to individual stocks and shares, detail is vital. Begin by documenting the stock ticker symbols for each company you have invested in. The ticker symbol is a unique identifier for each publicly traded company, such as AAPL for Apple Inc. Alongside the ticker symbol, record the number of shares you own. This information provides a snapshot of your holdings in each company. It's also important to note these stocks' purchase prices and dates. This data helps calculate capital gains or losses, which can have tax implications. For instance, if you bought 100 shares of Apple at $150 each on January 15, 2022, record these specifics.

Dividend payments are another critical aspect of documenting your investments. Dividends are payments made by companies to their shareholders, typically quarterly or annually. Record the frequency of these payments to keep track of your income from dividends. Note the amounts received each time and whether you have opted for reinvestment. Some investors choose to reinvest their dividends, buying more company shares, while others prefer to receive the payments as cash. Detailing this information helps you understand your income stream and how it contributes to your financial picture. For example, note this arrangement if you receive quarterly dividends of $200 from Apple and have chosen to reinvest them.

It's equally important to document your investment advisors and contacts. These professionals play a significant role in managing your investments and providing financial advice. List their names and contact information, including phone numbers and email addresses. Additionally, specify their roles and responsibilities. For instance, you might have a financial advisor who manages your overall portfolio and a tax advisor who helps with tax planning related to your investments. Keeping this information organized ensures that your loved ones know whom to contact for assistance and advice, maintaining continuity in managing your assets.

Call-to-Action: Organize Your Investment Portfolio

- List all brokerage firms and account details.
- Brokerage firm names
- Account numbers
- Types of investments (stocks, bonds, mutual funds)

- Document individual stocks and shares.
- Stock ticker symbols
- Number of shares owned
- Purchase prices and dates
- Record dividend payment details.
- Frequency of payments (quarterly, annually)
- Amounts received
- Reinvestment options
- List investment advisors and contacts.
- Names and contact information
- Roles and responsibilities

Taking the time to document your investments and stocks thoroughly ensures that your financial affairs are in order. This organization helps you manage your portfolio more effectively and provides clear guidance for your loved ones in the future. You create a comprehensive record that simplifies managing and distributing your investments by keeping track of every detail, from brokerage accounts to dividend payments. Your effort in organizing this information will provide invaluable support to those who will handle your financial legacy.

3.3 MANAGING DEBTS AND LIABILITIES

When managing your financial affairs, documenting all current debts is a crucial step. Start by listing each of your outstanding debts in detail. This includes credit card debts, personal loans, and mortgages. For credit card debts, note the issuing bank, the card type, and the current balance. For personal loans, document the lender's name, the original loan amount, and the remaining balance. Mortgages should include the lender, the property address, and the outstanding loan amount. This comprehensive list provides a clear view of your financial obligations, making managing them more accessible for you and your loved ones.

The next step is to detail payment schedules and amounts. For each debt, record the monthly payment amount, the due date, and the interest rate. This information is vital for keeping track of your financial commitments and ensuring timely payments. For instance, note these details clearly if you have a mortgage with a monthly fee of $1,500 due on the first of each month and an interest rate of 4%. Similarly, document this information if you have a credit card with a minimum payment of $100 due on the 15th of each month and an interest rate of 18%. Keeping track of these details helps you maintain financial discipline and avoid late fees or penalties.

Including contact information for creditors is equally essential. List each creditor's name, phone number, and account representative if applicable. This makes it easier for you or your loved ones to reach out to creditors if there are any issues or if further information is needed. For example, if you have a car loan with XYZ Bank, include the bank's contact number and the name of the loan officer handling your account. This readily available information ensures that any queries or concerns can be addressed promptly.

Planning for debt repayment after death is critical to managing your financial affairs. Consider providing detailed instructions for your executor regarding debt repayment. This includes specifying which debts should be paid off first and any special arrangements you have with certain creditors. For instance, you should prioritize paying off high-interest debts like credit cards before addressing lower-interest loans like mortgages. Additionally, if you have any debts co-signed with another person, ensure the executor knows these agreements. Clear instructions help your executor manage your estate efficiently and reduce the likelihood of financial complications.

In some cases, debts may be forgiven upon death, depending on the type of debt and the creditor's policies. However, this is not always the case, and it's essential to plan for the repayment of all outstanding obligations. Understanding the terms of each debt and discussing them with your creditors can clarify what to expect. For example, some student loans may be discharged upon death, while others may not. Knowing these details helps you make better decisions and plan more effectively.

Reflection Section: Assessing Your Debts

Take a moment to reflect on your current debts. Write down each debt's monthly payment, due date, and interest rate. Consider how these debts impact your overall financial situation. Are there any opportunities to consolidate or refinance your debts to lower your monthly payments or interest rates? Reflect on your plans for debt repayment and how you can ensure your financial obligations do not burden your loved ones.

Managing your debts and liabilities involves documenting all outstanding debts, detailing payment schedules, including creditor contact information, and planning for debt repayment after death. By taking these steps, you create a clear and organized record of your financial obligations, making it easier for you and your loved ones to manage them effectively. This proactive approach secures your financial future and provides peace of mind for your family.

3.4 INSURANCE POLICIES AND COVERAGE

Begin by listing all your insurance policies. This step is crucial in creating a comprehensive record of your coverage. Start with life insurance, a fundamental part of any financial plan. Document your policy type, whether term life or permanent life insurance. Term life insurance provides coverage for a specific period, like 10, 20, or 30 years, and pays a death benefit if you die during the term.

On the other hand, permanent life insurance offers lifelong coverage and includes a cash value component. Including both types ensures your loved ones understand the scope of your coverage. Next, list your health insurance policies. These could include Medicare, supplemental insurance, or private health insurance plans. Lastly, document your homeowner's insurance, which protects your property and possessions. This step ensures that all your bases are covered and provides a clear picture of your insurance landscape.

Recording specific policy details is essential for clarity and ease of access. Start with the policy numbers for each insurance policy. These unique identifiers are crucial for filing claims or making changes to your policy. Equally important are the coverage limits, which detail the maximum amount the insurer will pay under your policy. For life insurance, this is the death benefit amount. For health insurance, it includes coverage for medical expenses. For homeowner's insurance, it covers the replacement cost of your home and belongings. Also, note the premium payment schedules. Knowing when your premiums are due helps ensure that your policies remain active. For example, if your life insurance premium is due annually in January, note this. Detailed records of your policy specifics ensure that you and your loved ones have all the necessary information at your fingertips.

Include contact information for your insurance agents. These professionals are your go-to resources for any questions or issues related to your policies. List their names and contact numbers, along with their roles and responsibilities. For instance, your life insurance agent might be responsible for policy updates and claims processing, while your health insurance agent might handle medical claims and coverage questions. This readily available contact information ensures that you or your loved ones can quickly reach out for assistance. This step simplifies communication and ensures that your insurance matters are handled efficiently.

Documenting the claims processes and beneficiaries for each policy is equally important. Start with the steps for filing a claim. This includes the necessary forms, supporting documentation, and the contact information for the claims department. Life insurance might involve providing a death certificate and completing a claim form. For health insurance, it could include submitting medical bills and claim forms. Clearly outlining these steps ensures your loved ones can navigate the claims process smoothly. Next, list the beneficiaries for each insurance policy. These are the individuals or entities who will receive the benefits from your policy. For life insurance, this might be your spouse or children. For homeowner's insurance, it could be yourself or your mortgage lender. Identifying the beneficiaries ensures that the benefits are distributed according to your wishes.

For instance, consider a scenario where you have a term life insurance policy with a $500,000 death benefit. Your spouse is the primary beneficiary, and your children are contingent beneficiaries. Document the policy number, coverage amount, and premium payment schedule. Include the contact information for your insurance agent, who can assist with filing claims. Detail the steps for filing a claim, such as providing a death certificate and completing the necessary forms. This level of detail ensures that your loved ones can access the benefits without unnecessary delays or complications.

Taking these steps to document your insurance policies and coverage creates a comprehensive record that simplifies the management of your financial affairs. It ensures that you and your loved ones have all the necessary information to navigate the complexities of insurance coverage. By listing all your policies, recording specific details, including agent contacts, and documenting the claims processes and beneficiaries, you provide a clear and organized approach to managing your insurance affairs. This preparation ensures that your coverage is maintained and provides peace of mind for you and your loved ones.

3.5 REAL ESTATE AND PROPERTY DOCUMENTATION

Documenting all your properties is a fundamental part of organizing your financial affairs. Start by listing each property you own, including the complete addresses. It is crucial to note the exact location of your primary residence, a vacation home, or an investment property. For example, write down each address if you own a house at 123 Maple Street and a condo at 456 Oak Avenue. This level of detail helps create a comprehensive record of your real estate holdings, ensuring everything is noticed. Additionally, specify the types of properties, whether they are residential, commercial, or even agricultural. This differentiation is essential for understanding the nature and use of each property, which can affect its value and how it is managed.

Mortgage information is another critical element to document. Start with the names of the lenders for each property. Knowing who holds the mortgage is essential for managing payments and addressing any issues that might arise. Next, record the current loan balances. This information clearly shows how much is still owed on each property. Alongside the balances, include the payment schedules. Note when payments are due, whether monthly, quarterly, or annually. This helps ensure timely payments are made, avoiding late fees or penalties. Also, document the interest rates for each mortgage. Understanding these rates is essential for managing your finances and planning for future payments. For instance, if you have a mortgage with a 3.5% interest rate due on the 15th of each month, note these specifics to keep everything organized.

Having property deeds and titles readily accessible is vital for verifying ownership and managing your real estate. Start by identifying the locations of the original documents. These might be stored in a safe deposit box, a home safe, or with your attorney. Knowing where these documents are ensures they can be accessed quickly. Having copies of these documents for reference is also a good idea. Copies can be kept in a separate location or digitized for easy access. This redundancy ensures that even if the original documents are lost or damaged, you still have the information to prove ownership and manage the properties effectively.

Property tax information is another crucial aspect to document. Start by recording the annual property tax amounts for each property. This information helps you understand your tax obligations and plan your budget accordingly. Alongside the tax amounts, note the payment due dates. Property taxes are typically annually owing or semi-annually; keeping track of these dates ensures that payments are made on time. Late payments can result in penalties or interest charges, so staying on top of these due dates is essential.

Additionally, include the contact information for the tax assessor's office responsible for each property. Knowing whom to contact for tax-related questions or issues simplifies the process of managing your property taxes. For example, if your property tax for 123 Maple Street is $3,000, due every June, document this clearly, along with the assessor's contact details.

By documenting your real estate and property details, you create a clear and organized record that simplifies the management of these assets. Listing all properties, including mortgage information, having deeds and titles accessible, and recording property tax details ensures that you and your loved ones have a comprehensive understanding of your real estate holdings. This preparation helps manage your properties effectively and provides peace of mind, knowing that all necessary information is readily available.

3.6 HANDLING RETIREMENT ACCOUNTS

When handling your retirement accounts, the first step is to list all accounts you hold. This includes 401(k) accounts, IRAs (both traditional and Roth), and pension plans. Document each account in detail, including the account number and the financial institution where it is held. For instance, if you have a 401(k) with Fidelity and an IRA with Vanguard, clearly note these details. Recording this information helps ensure that your loved ones can quickly locate and manage these accounts when the time comes. This comprehensive list serves as a roadmap for your financial future, providing clarity and organization.

Next, detailing each retirement account's account balances and contributions is essential. Gather the most recent annual statements summarizing your account activity over the past year. These statements typically include the current balance, contributions made during the year, and any investment gains or losses. Also, note the contribution limits for each account type. For example, the IRS sets annual contribution limits for 401(k) and IRA accounts, which can change yearly. Documenting these limits helps you maximize your contributions and take full advantage of tax-deferred growth. Include details about the employer match for your 401(k). If your employer matches 5% of your salary, this is valuable information to record, as it significantly impacts your retirement savings.

Including beneficiary information for each retirement account is crucial. Make sure to list the names and contact information of your beneficiaries. This could be your spouse, children, or other loved ones. Specify the percentage each beneficiary will receive. For instance, you allocate 50% of your 401(k) to your spouse and 25% each to your two children. This clear designation ensures that your retirement assets are distributed according to your wishes. Beneficiary designations override your will, so it's essential to keep them updated, especially after significant life events like marriage, divorce, or the birth of a child. Keeping this information current prevents legal complications and ensures that your loved ones receive their intended share promptly.

Another critical aspect is understanding your retirement account's withdrawal rules and penalties. Document the age requirements for accessing these funds without incurring penalties. You can start taking distributions without penalty at age 59½ for most retirement accounts. However, Required Minimum Distributions (RMDs) begin at age 72 for most accounts, requiring you to withdraw a certain amount each year. Note these age requirements and any early withdrawal penalties that may apply if you access the funds before the specified age. For instance, early withdrawals from a traditional IRA before age 59½ typically incur a 10% penalty in addition to regular income tax. Detailing these rules helps you plan your withdrawals strategically, minimizing penalties and maximizing your retirement income.

Consider a scenario where you have multiple retirement

accounts, including a 401(k) balance of $200,000, a traditional IRA with $150,000, and a pension plan that provides monthly payments. Documenting the account balances, contribution histories, and beneficiary information for each account ensures that your financial picture is clear and organized. Additionally, noting the withdrawal rules and penalties helps you plan for future distributions, ensuring that you can access your funds when needed without unnecessary costs. This thorough documentation provides a solid foundation for managing your retirement accounts effectively now and in the future.

Taking these steps to handle your retirement accounts ensures that your financial affairs are well-organized and easily accessible. Listing all retirement accounts, detailing account balances and contributions, including beneficiary information, and understanding withdrawal rules and penalties provides a comprehensive overview of your retirement savings. This preparation secures your financial future and gives you and your loved ones peace of mind. By keeping this information current and well-documented, you create a clear and organized record that simplifies the management of your retirement assets. Your effort in handling these accounts ensures that your retirement savings are maximized and distributed according to your wishes, supporting your financial goals and those of your loved ones.

4
DIGITAL AND ONLINE PRESENCE

Our digital presence, from email to social media, is as significant as our physical documents. This chapter will guide you through organizing your digital life, ensuring that your passwords and online accounts are secure and accessible for you and your loved ones.

4.1 ORGANIZING YOUR PASSWORDS

In today's digital age, passwords are more important than ever. Keeping your passwords organized is crucial for digital security and accessibility. Unauthorized access to your accounts can lead to identity theft, financial loss, and other problems. By maintaining a well-organized system, you can prevent these issues. Moreover, ensuring that your loved ones can access important accounts in emergencies is equally vital. Imagine your family needing access to your financial accounts or important documents but unable to do so because they don't know the passwords. Proper password management can prevent such scenarios, providing you and your loved ones peace of mind.

Creating a password inventory is the first step toward achieving this goal. Different ways to do this depend on your comfort level with technology. One effective method is using a password manager. These tools securely store all your passwords in one place, accessible through a single master password. Password managers like 1Password or Bit warden offer features such as password hygiene alerts and secure sharing options. You can opt for manual documentation if you're uncomfortable using digital tools. Create a comprehensive list of your passwords and store it securely, such as an encrypted document or a physical notebook in a locked drawer. Whichever method you choose, ensure that your inventory includes all necessary details, such as usernames, passwords, and any security questions associated with your accounts.

Updating and maintaining your passwords is an ongoing task that is crucial for security. Regularly updating your passwords reduces the risk of unauthorized access. Set reminders to change your passwords periodically, ideally every three to six months. This habit ensures the damage is limited even if a password is compromised. Use strong, unique passwords for each account. A strong password typically includes a combination of letters, numbers, and special characters, making it harder to crack. Avoid using easily guessable information, such as birthdays or common words. Password managers can generate strong passwords for you, adding an extra layer of security. You significantly enhance your digital security by maintaining a routine of updating your passwords and using solid combinations.

Sharing passwords securely with trusted individuals is another important aspect of password management. There are several methods to do this safely. Secure password-sharing tools, such as those offered by password managers, allow you to share passwords without revealing them directly. These tools ensure that only the intended recipient can access the shared information. Alternatively, you can provide sealed, written copies of your passwords to trusted family members. Store these copies in a safe place, such as a locked drawer or safe deposit box, and inform your family members about their existence and location. Avoid sharing passwords through insecure channels like email or text messages, as these methods can be easily intercepted.

Call-to-Action: Secure Your Digital Life

- Utilize a password manager to store and organize your passwords securely.
- If you prefer manual documentation, create a comprehensive list and store it in a secure format.
- Set reminders to update your passwords every three to six months.
- Use strong, unique passwords for each account, avoiding easily guessable information.
- Share passwords securely through password managers or by providing sealed, written copies to trusted family members.

By following these steps, you can ensure your digital presence is secure and accessible. Proper password management protects you from unauthorized access and provides peace of mind, knowing that your loved ones can access important accounts when needed. Taking these proactive measures secures your digital life and supports the overall organization of your end-of-life planning.

4.2 DOCUMENTING SOCIAL MEDIA ACCOUNTS

In today's interconnected world, social media platforms play a significant role. They are tools for staying in touch with friends and family and repositories of cherished memories and essential communications. To ensure that your digital presence is managed according to your wishes, it is crucial to document all your social media accounts. Start by listing all your platforms, such as Facebook, X, and Instagram. For each platform, note down your username and the associated email address. This information provides a clear record of your digital footprint, making it easier for your loved ones to manage your accounts when necessary.

Once you have listed your social media profiles, the next step is to outline your preferences for managing these accounts after passing. Each platform offers different options for account management. For instance, Facebook allows you to request account deactivation or set up a memorialization setting that turns your profile into a tribute page. Think about what you want to happen to each of your accounts. Do you want them deactivated, memorialized, or left as they are? Document these preferences clearly, providing specific instructions for each platform. This clarity ensures that your wishes are respected and that your digital legacy is managed to align with your values.

Another critical step is providing access information for your social media accounts. Ensure you include all necessary login details, such as usernames, passwords, security questions, or two-factor authentication methods. This information is crucial for allowing your designated person to access and manage your accounts. With these details, your loved ones might be able to follow your wishes, leading to potential complications and frustration. By documenting this information, you make it easier for them to handle your social media presence efficiently and according to your instructions.

It is also essential to inform your family and friends about your social media wishes. Open a conversation with your close family members and discuss your preferences for managing your accounts. Designate a digital executor, someone you trust to handle your digital assets according to your wishes. This person should be tech-savvy and understand your values. Communicate your preferences for public and private content, ensuring they know which posts, photos, or messages you want to remain visible and which should be removed. This discussion provides clarity and ensures that your digital presence is managed respectfully and thoughtfully.

Checklist: Documenting Social Media Accounts

- List all social media platforms you use, such as Facebook, X, and Instagram.
- Include usernames and associated email addresses for each platform.
- Outline your preferences for account management after you pass.
- Specify whether you want accounts deactivated, memorialized, or left unchanged.
- Provide access information for each account.
- Include usernames, passwords, and any security questions or two-factor authentication methods.
- Inform your family and friends about your social media wishes.
- Designate a digital executor who will manage your digital assets.
- Communicate preferences for public and private content.

By taking these steps to document and manage your social media accounts, you ensure that your digital presence is handled according to your wishes. This preparation protects your online legacy and provides peace of mind for you and your loved ones, knowing that your social media profiles will be managed respectfully and thoughtfully.

4.3 MANAGING EMAIL ACCOUNTS

One of the first steps in organizing your digital presence is documenting all your email accounts. Many of us have multiple email addresses for different purposes. Start by listing your primary email accounts. You often use these email addresses for personal communication and essential notifications. For example, you might have a primary email with Gmail or Yahoo. Next, document any secondary or backup emails. These accounts might be used for less critical communications or as a fallback if your primary account has issues.

Additionally, include any work-related emails if you are still employed or have had a professional career. Listing all these accounts provides a comprehensive overview, ensuring every email account is noticed.

Providing login details for each email account is crucial for accessibility. Make sure to include the email addresses themselves, as well as the passwords. This information is essential for accessing the accounts and managing your emails. Don't forget to document any security questions associated with these accounts. Many email providers use security questions as an additional layer of protection. Knowing the answers to these questions can be crucial if you or your loved ones need to recover a forgotten password. Providing all this information ensures that your email accounts can be accessed without unnecessary hurdles.

Setting up email forwarding or auto-responses is a practical way to handle ongoing communications, especially if you anticipate being unable to manage your emails for a period. Email forwarding involves configuring your email account to forward incoming messages to a trusted person automatically. This way, essential emails are noticed, and your designated person can handle any necessary replies. Auto-responses, on the other hand, are automated messages sent to anyone who emails you, informing them that you might be unable to respond immediately. For instance, you can set up an auto-response stating, "Thank you for your email. I am currently unavailable and may not be able to respond promptly." These tools ensure that your correspondents are informed and critical communications are managed appropriately.

You are guiding your loved ones in handling your email accounts after your passing, which is another important consideration. Specify your preferences for email account management, such as whether you want the accounts deleted or archived. Deleting accounts involves permanently removing them, along with all associated emails and data. This option might be suitable if you prefer that your digital footprint be minimized. On the other hand, archiving important emails preserves them for future reference. Archiving can be particularly useful for emails containing valuable information, such as financial statements or personal correspondences. Provide precise steps for each option, ensuring that your loved ones can follow your instructions easily. Additionally, inform key contacts about your email account deactivation. This step prevents confusion and ensures that people know how to reach out to your designated person if needed.

Managing your email accounts is a crucial part of organizing your digital presence. Documenting all email accounts, providing necessary login details, setting up forwarding or auto-responses, and specifying preferences for account management ensures that your emails are handled efficiently and according to your wishes. This thorough approach secures your digital communications and provides clarity and ease for your loved ones, allowing them to manage your email accounts without unnecessary stress.

4.4 HANDLING ONLINE SUBSCRIPTIONS AND SERVICES

Managing your online subscriptions and services is essential to organizing your digital life. Start by documenting all your online subscriptions. This includes streaming services like Netflix and Hulu, which provide entertainment at your fingertips. Don't forget about online memberships such as Amazon Prime, which offer benefits like free shipping and access to exclusive content. Additionally, list any digital news and magazine subscriptions you have. These include subscriptions to The New York Times, National Geographic, or other publications you enjoy. By listing all these services, you create a comprehensive overview of your digital commitments, making them easier to manage.

Including payment information for each of these services is crucial. Document the credit card details associated with each subscription, including the card number, expiration date, and security code. This information ensures that you or your loved ones can easily update or cancel subscriptions. Also, note the billing cycles for each service. Some subscriptions might bill monthly, while others might be annual. Knowing these cycles helps you anticipate charges and manage your finances more effectively. Finally, include the renewal dates for each subscription. This detail is essential for planning, as it lets you decide whether to continue or cancel a service before it renews automatically.

Setting up cancellation instructions for your subscriptions is another crucial step. Each service will have its process for canceling, so document the specific steps required for each one. Start by visiting the service's website and looking for the account settings or subscription management section. There, you will typically find an option to cancel your subscription. Note any steps involved, such as confirming the cancellation through an email link or providing a reason for canceling.

Additionally, include the contact information for customer support. This can be helpful if you encounter any issues during the cancellation process. For example, if you need to cancel your Netflix subscription, include instructions on navigating to the account settings and the customer support number for assistance.

If you wish to transfer or hand over your subscriptions to someone else, there are a few steps to follow. First, consider changing the account ownership. Many services allow you to update the account details to reflect a new owner. This might involve changing the name, email address, and payment information associated with the account. Sharing login details with a trusted family member is another option. Provide them with the username and password, ensuring they can access the service. Specify which services you want to maintain and which ones can be canceled. For instance, keep an Amazon Prime membership active for its benefits but cancel other subscriptions that no longer need renewal. Clear instructions make the process seamless for your loved ones.

Consider the case of a retiree who subscribes to multiple online services. They have Netflix for streaming movies, Amazon Prime for shopping and entertainment, and The Wall Street Journal for daily news. They record their digital commitments clearly by documenting each subscription, including payment information and renewal dates. They also set up cancellation instructions for each service, detailing the steps to follow and providing customer support contact information. Additionally, they specify that the Amazon Prime membership should be transferred to their spouse, while other subscriptions can be canceled. This meticulous documentation ensures that their digital life is managed smoothly, providing peace of mind for themselves and their loved ones.

Managing your online subscriptions and services involves documenting all subscriptions, providing payment information, setting up cancellation instructions, and offering advice on transferring or handing over accounts. By taking these steps, you ensure that your digital commitments are organized and easily accessible. This preparation helps you manage your finances more effectively and provides clarity and ease for your loved ones, allowing them to handle your online subscriptions without unnecessary stress.

4.5 DIGITAL LEGACY PLANNING

Understanding your digital legacy is just as important as managing your physical assets. A digital legacy encompasses all the digital content you create and interact with during your life. This includes emails, social media profiles, digital photos, videos, and any online blogs or personal websites you may have. Preserving these digital memories ensures that your life's story remains accessible to your loved ones. Managing your online presence after death involves deciding how these digital assets should be handled and whether they should be archived, shared, or deleted. This planning helps prevent your digital footprint from becoming a burden or a source of confusion for your family.

Appointing a digital executor is a critical step in managing your digital legacy. This trusted individual will carry out your digital wishes, much like an executor handles your physical estate. The roles and responsibilities of a digital executor include accessing your online accounts, managing or deleting digital content, and ensuring that your digital presence is handled according to your wishes. Legal considerations are essential when appointing a digital executor, as different platforms have varying policies regarding account access after death. In your will, clearly state who your digital executor is and provide them with the necessary permissions to manage your digital assets. This legal backing ensures they can act on your behalf without facing obstacles.

Creating a clear plan for your digital assets involves documenting each aspect of your online life. Start with your social media accounts, listing each platform, username, and password. This documentation allows your digital executor to access and manage these accounts seamlessly. Next, consider your digital photos and videos. These often hold sentimental value and should be preserved carefully. Specify whether you want these memories archived, shared with specific family members, or deleted. For online blogs and personal websites, outline your preferences for managing these. You may want them to remain accessible as a testament to your work, or you might prefer them to be taken down. Providing detailed instructions for each digital asset ensures your wishes are honored.

Several tools and services can assist in managing your digital legacy. The Google Inactive Account Manager is one such tool. It allows you to decide what happens to your Google account data if your account becomes inactive for a specified period. You can share your data with a trusted contact or delete it. Setting this up is straightforward—visit the Google Inactive Account Manager page, select the inactivity period, and designate your trusted contact.

Similarly, Facebook offers the Legacy Contact feature, allowing you to appoint someone to manage your account after you pass away. Your legacy contact can write a pinned post, respond to friend requests, and update your profile picture. These tools provide a structured way to manage your digital legacy, ensuring your online presence is handled according to your wishes.

Digital legacy planning services offer another layer of support. These services specialize in helping you organize and manage your digital assets. They provide templates, guidelines, and secure storage options for your digital information. Utilizing these services ensures that every aspect of your digital legacy is covered, from social media to personal photographs. They also offer peace of mind, knowing that professionals are assisting in preserving your digital footprint.

Understanding your digital legacy and taking steps to manage it ensures that your digital presence reflects your wishes. Appointing a digital executor, creating a detailed plan for your digital assets, and using available tools and services provide a comprehensive approach to digital legacy planning. This preparation preserves your digital memories and provides clarity and support for your loved ones, ensuring that your digital life is managed respectfully and thoughtfully.

4.6 TIPS FOR SECURING DIGITAL INFORMATION

In today's interconnected world, digital security is not just a luxury but a necessity. Protecting your digital information from unauthorized access is crucial for preventing identity theft and safeguarding personal data. When someone gains access to your sensitive information, they can misuse it in various harmful ways, from draining your bank accounts to opening new lines of credit in your name. The consequences can be devastating and long-lasting. Therefore, it is essential to implement robust security measures to protect your digital assets. This involves a combination of strong passwords, two-factor authentication, regular updates, and educating your family about best practices.

Strong passwords are one of the most effective ways to secure digital information. A strong password should be unique and complex, combining letters, numbers, and special characters. Avoid using easily guessable information such as your name, birthdate, or common words. Passwords like "12345" or "password" are vulnerable to hacking attempts. Instead, opt for a mix of upper and lowercase letters, numbers, and symbols. For example, a strong password might look like "G4$h!9kL!7". Enabling two-factor authentication (2FA) adds an extra layer of security. This method requires a password and a second verification form, such as a code sent to your mobile phone. Many online services, including email providers and social media platforms, offer 2FA as an option. Enabling this feature can significantly reduce the risk of unauthorized access.

Keeping your security measures current is another crucial aspect of digital security. Periodically changing your passwords helps minimize the risk of them being compromised. Set reminders to update your passwords every few months. This practice ensures that even if a password is leaked, the window of opportunity for misuse is limited. Additionally, regularly update your software and security patches. Whether it's your operating system, web browser, or any other software, keeping everything up-to-date ensures you have the latest security features and protections. Software updates often include patches for newly discovered vulnerabilities that hackers could exploit. Stay current, close these security gaps, and protect your digital information more effectively.

Educating your family members about digital security practices is equally important. Share best practices for online safety with them, ensuring they understand the importance of strong passwords, two-factor authentication, and regular updates. For instance, explain why they should avoid clicking on suspicious links or downloading unknown attachments, as these can be vectors for malware and phishing attacks. Providing resources for further learning can also be helpful. Please direct them to reputable websites or online courses that offer detailed information about digital security. By fostering a culture of awareness and vigilance, you help protect your digital assets and those of your loved ones.

In summary, securing your digital information involves using strong passwords, enabling two-factor authentication, regularly updating security measures, and educating your family about best practices. These steps help prevent identity theft and safeguard personal data, providing peace of mind in today's digital age. As we move forward, the next chapter will guide you through organizing essential documents and locations, ensuring that your affairs are in order and easily accessible for your loved ones.

HELP OTHERS PLAN FOR THE FUTURE

"If you fail to plan, you are planning to fail!"

— BENJAMIN FRANKLIN

At this point in your reading journey, think about the many ways you have already started to plan for both your and your family's future. You have already taken a big step toward the peace of mind that comes with knowing that your loved ones know and can respect your wishes. And you will know you have done your best to care for them.

Take a moment and consider this: if you are enjoying your read thus far, others may benefit from your experience. Please take half a minute to let others know.

By leaving a review of this book on Amazon, you'll let new readers know that planning for the inevitable is not overwhelming and can be done with a little time and attention. Just scan the QR code below:

Thanks for your help. Ready to discover how good it feels to know you have a plan? Let's continue to Chapter 5.

5
MEDICAL INFORMATION AND HEALTH CARE

Documenting your medical history helps you manage your health better and provides crucial details to your healthcare providers and loved ones. This chapter will guide you through gathering, documenting, and maintaining a thorough medical history.

5.1 RECORDING YOUR MEDICAL HISTORY

The first step in creating an accurate medical history is gathering comprehensive medical records. Start by requesting your health records from various sources. Hospitals, primary care physicians, and specialists all hold pieces of your medical puzzle. You can access some of this information through online patient portals, which many providers offer. If your required information is not available online, you may need to visit the provider's office or call to request it. The HIPAA Privacy Rule ensures your right to access your health records, and providers must comply within 30 days. You may need to fill out a medical record release form, and while providers can charge a reasonable fee for copies, they cannot deny you access due to unpaid bills. Ensuring you have all relevant records from different healthcare providers gives you a comprehensive view of your medical history.

Once you have collected your records, the next step is to document your health events chronologically. Start with past surgeries, listing the dates and outcomes. Include any significant illnesses, such as heart attacks or strokes, and detail the treatments you received. Chronic conditions like diabetes or hypertension should also be noted, along with how they are managed. Documenting these events in order helps create a clear timeline of your health, making it easier for healthcare providers to understand your medical journey. This chronological approach also enables you to track the progression of conditions and the effectiveness of treatments over time.

Including family medical history is equally important. Family history is a significant factor in the risk of developing conditions like heart disease, stroke, diabetes, and cancer. Shared genes, environment, and lifestyle within families contribute to health risks. Key features that increase disease risk include diseases occurring earlier than usual, diseases in multiple close relatives, and diseases affecting unusual genders. For example, breast cancer in males or combinations of diseases like breast and ovarian cancer within the family can indicate a higher risk. This information involves talking to relatives, reviewing death certificates, and examining medical records. Collect details about primary medical conditions, causes of death, age of disease onset, and ethnic background. Sharing this information with your doctor can help them assess your disease risk and recommend preventive measures.

Providing context for medical conditions is crucial for understanding their impact on daily life. Start by detailing any limitations or restrictions caused by your conditions. For instance, if arthritis limits mobility, note how it affects your daily activities. Include any required accommodations, such as the need for assistive devices or modifications to your home. Understanding these limitations helps healthcare providers offer appropriate support and interventions. It also informs your loved ones about the practical implications of your conditions.

Additionally, describe the overall impact on your quality of life. Chronic pain, fatigue, or emotional challenges can significantly affect your well-being. Providing this context ensures that your healthcare team has a holistic view of your health, enabling them to offer more personalized and effective care.

Gathering, documenting, and contextualizing your medical history is comprehensive but essential for effective healthcare management. Start by requesting health records from various providers and documenting health events chronologically. Include a detailed family medical history to help assess your risk for inherited conditions. Provide context for your medical conditions to illustrate their impact on your daily life and quality of life. This holistic approach ensures that your healthcare providers and loved ones clearly and thoroughly understand your health, enabling better care and support.

Checklist: Comprehensive Medical History

- Gather records from hospitals, primary care physicians, and specialists.
- Document past surgeries, major illnesses, and chronic conditions in chronological order.
- Include family medical history, noting hereditary conditions and predispositions.
- Provide context for medical conditions, detailing limitations, required accommodations, and impact on quality of life.

5.2 DOCUMENTING CURRENT MEDICATIONS

You likely have a variety of medications that you take regularly. Keeping a detailed list of these medications is crucial for your health and safety. Start by documenting all the prescription medications you are currently taking. Include the name of each medication, the dosage, and the prescribing doctor. This information provides a clear picture of your treatment plan and helps healthcare providers avoid prescribing medicines that might interact negatively with what you are already taking.

In addition to prescription medications, don't forget to list over-the-counter drugs. These can include pain relievers, allergy medications, and other non-prescription drugs you use regularly. Many people overlook these, but they can have significant interactions with prescription medications. Supplements and vitamins should also be documented. While these are often considered harmless, they can interact with drugs or affect your health unexpectedly. You provide a complete picture of your health regimen by listing everything you take.

Detailing dosages and schedules is essential. For each medication, note the exact dosage amount, the frequency of doses, and the times you take them. For example, you might take 50 mg of a blood pressure medication twice a day, once in the morning and once in the evening. Being specific about these details helps ensure that anyone assisting with your care can administer your medications correctly. It also helps healthcare providers understand your treatment plan and make necessary adjustments.

Understanding the purpose and potential side effects of each medication is equally important. For every medication on your list, include the condition it is treating. For instance, you might take a statin to manage high cholesterol or an anticoagulant to prevent blood clots. Knowing the purpose helps you and your healthcare team monitor the effectiveness of your treatment. Additionally, note common side effects and any interactions with other medications. This information can be crucial in identifying the cause of new symptoms or adverse reactions. For example, a statin might cause muscle pain, or an anticoagulant might increase the risk of bleeding.

Awareness of these side effects allows you to address them promptly with your healthcare provider.

Regularly updating your medication list is vital for maintaining its accuracy. Your medications can change frequently due to new prescriptions, discontinued drugs, or dosage adjustments. Each time there is a change, update your list immediately. Remove any medications you are no longer taking and add new ones as prescribed. Keeping this list current ensures that anyone involved in your care has the most accurate information. It also helps prevent mistakes, such as taking an outdated medication or missing a new one.

Consider using a digital tool or a simple notebook to keep track of your medications. A digital tool can offer reminders for when to take your medications and prompts to update your list. If you prefer a physical notebook, ensure it is easily accessible and updated regularly. Sharing this list with your primary care physician, specialists, and even trusted family members can be incredibly beneficial. It ensures everyone involved in your care is on the same page and can act swiftly and accurately in an emergency.

Checklist: Documenting Current Medications

- List all prescription medications, including names, dosages, and prescribing doctors.
- Include over-the-counter drugs, noting their specific uses and dosages.
- Document all supplements and vitamins, detailing their intended benefits.
- Record the exact dosage amounts, frequency of doses, and times of day for each medication.
- Note the purpose of each medication, the condition it treats, and any common side effects or interactions.
- Regularly update your medication list whenever there are changes, adding new medications and removing discontinued ones.

- Share your updated medication list with your healthcare providers and trusted family members for comprehensive care management.

By taking these steps, you ensure that your medication management is thorough and effective, providing a clear roadmap for you and your healthcare team. This detailed approach minimizes risks and maximizes the benefits of your treatment, ensuring your health and safety.

5.3 CONTACT INFORMATION FOR HEALTHCARE PROVIDERS

A complete list of your healthcare providers is crucial for managing your health effectively. Start by documenting your primary care physicians. Include their full names, contact numbers, and office addresses. This information ensures that you or your loved ones can quickly contact your healthcare provider for routine check-ups or medical concerns. For instance, your primary care physician might be Dr. Jane Smith, reachable at (555) 123-4567, with an office at 123 Health Street. Keeping this information easily accessible helps streamline communication and ensures you receive timely care.

In addition to your primary care provider, it's essential to list all specialists and therapists involved in your care. Specialists like cardiologists, neurologists, and oncologists play a significant role in managing specific health conditions. Document their names, contact numbers, and office addresses as well. For example, you might have Dr. John Doe, a cardiologist whose office is at 456 Heart Avenue, and can be contacted at (555) 987-6543. Similarly, it includes information for physical therapists and mental health professionals. Physical therapists help manage mobility and pain, while mental health professionals, such as psychologists and counselors, support your emotional well-being. This comprehensive list ensures that all aspects of your health are covered and that you can easily connect with the right specialist when needed.

Emergency contact information is another vital component. Documenting the nearest hospital emergency departments ensures that you or your loved ones know where to go in a medical emergency. Include the hospital name, address, and emergency department contact number. For example, the nearest hospital might be General Health Hospital, located at 789 Emergency Lane, with a contact number of (555) 321-9876. Additionally, list on-call doctors and urgent care centers. On-call doctors can provide immediate medical advice, while urgent care centers are suitable for non-life-threatening conditions requiring prompt attention. Including this information helps you make quick decisions during emergencies and ensures you receive the appropriate level of care.

Pharmacy information is equally important. Document your preferred pharmacies, including their names, contact numbers, and specific details about prescription refill processes. For instance, you might use HealthFirst Pharmacy, which can be contacted at (555) 654-3210. Knowing the pharmacy's refill process is helpful; some pharmacies offer online refills, automatic refills, or delivery services. This information ensures you never miss a medication refill and can manage your prescriptions efficiently. It lets your healthcare providers quickly send prescriptions to the right place, ensuring you receive your medications without unnecessary delays.

Checklist: Contact Information for Healthcare Providers

- List primary care physicians with names, contact numbers, and office addresses.
- Include specialists and therapists, noting their fields, contact details, and office locations.
- Document emergency contact information for the nearest hospital emergency departments, on-call doctors, and urgent care centers.

- Provide information detailing preferred pharmacies, contact numbers, and prescription refill processes.

You create a robust support network for your healthcare needs by meticulously documenting this information. This comprehensive approach ensures that all relevant contact details are at your fingertips, enabling you to manage your health proactively and efficiently. Keeping this information updated and easily accessible provides peace of mind, knowing that you can swiftly connect with the necessary healthcare providers whenever needed.

5.4 HEALTH INSURANCE DETAILS

Health insurance is a cornerstone of managing your healthcare costs and ensuring you receive the necessary treatments without financial strain. It's crucial to document all health insurance policies you hold. Start by listing the provider names for each policy. For instance, you might have a Medicare plan, a supplemental insurance policy from AARP, and a private insurance policy through Blue Cross Blue Shield. Include the policy numbers, which are essential for identification, and the coverage start and end dates. This information provides a clear overview of your insurance landscape, making it easier to manage and reference when needed.

Understanding what each policy covers is vital for making informed decisions about your healthcare. Begin by detailing the coverage for inpatient and outpatient care. Inpatient care refers to treatments requiring a hospital stay, while outpatient care includes treatments not requiring hospitalization, such as doctor visits and minor procedures. Knowing what is covered under each category helps you avoid unexpected bills. Next, document the prescription drug coverage. This includes which medications are covered, the copays, and any limitations or restrictions. Preventive care benefits are another essential aspect to note. These benefits often cover routine screenings, vaccinations, and annual check-ups at no additional cost. A thorough understanding of your coverage ensures you can maximize your benefits and receive the care you need without unnecessary costs.

Equally important is having contact information for your insurers readily available. List the customer service numbers for each provider. These numbers are your first point of contact for any questions or issues with your policies. Additionally, include the claims department contacts. This information is crucial for filing claims or resolving disputes. Many insurance providers also offer online portals for managing policies. Document the URLs and your login information for these portals. These online tools allow you to review your coverage, file claims, and update your information from the comfort of your home. Keeping this contact information organized ensures you can quickly reach out for assistance.

Filing a claim can be a complex process, but having step-by-step instructions can simplify it. Start by listing the required documents for each type of claim. For example, filing a medical claim might need a copy of the bill, a completed claim form, and any relevant medical records. Submission deadlines are crucial to note. Missing a deadline can result in a denied claim, so knowing these timelines helps ensure your claims are processed promptly. Follow-up procedures are also necessary. After submitting a claim, record the submission date and any reference numbers provided. If you are still waiting for a response within a reasonable time, follow up with the claims department, providing the reference number to track your claim's status. Documenting these procedures ensures you can navigate the claims process efficiently, reducing stress and ensuring you receive the benefits you're entitled to.

Mary, a retiree, once shared her experience of struggling with an unexpected medical bill. She had undergone a routine procedure, believing her insurance entirely covered it. However, she later received a substantial bill. Reviewing her policy details, she discovered she had missed filing the claim within the specified timeframe while the procedure was covered. This oversight resulted in a denied claim. Mary realized the importance of understanding her policy coverage and the claims process. She now records all her insurance policies, coverage details, and step-by-step instructions for filing claims. This proactive approach ensures she avoids similar issues in the future and can manage her healthcare costs more effectively.

By thoroughly documenting your health insurance policies, understanding your coverage, and keeping insurer contact information and claim filing procedures at your fingertips, you ensure that you can effectively manage your healthcare needs. This organized approach helps you make the most of your insurance benefits and provides peace of mind, knowing that you are well-prepared to handle any medical expenses or issues that may arise.

5.5 PLANNING FOR LONG-TERM CARE

Navigating the landscape of long-term care begins with evaluating your specific needs. Start by assessing the daily living assistance you might require. This includes help with activities such as bathing, dressing, and eating. Consider your current abilities and anticipate how they may change over time. Medical and nursing care requirements are another critical aspect. If you have chronic conditions or anticipate needing medical treatments, factor these into your planning. Home modifications, such as installing grab bars or ramps, can make your living environment safer and more accessible. Evaluating these needs ensures you have a clear picture of the support you might require, helping you make informed decisions about your long-term care.

Once you understand your needs, explore the various types of long-term care available. In-home care services are an excellent option for those who prefer to stay home. Depending on your needs, these services can range from personal care aides to skilled nursing care. Assisted living facilities offer a middle ground, providing a community environment with assistance for daily activities while allowing a degree of independence. On the other hand, nursing homes provide comprehensive medical and personal care suitable for those with significant health issues. Understanding these options helps you choose the care setting that best aligns with your preferences and requirements.

Documenting your long-term care preferences is essential for ensuring your wishes are respected. Start by detailing your preferred care settings. For instance, utilizing in-home care services, you choose to remain at home for as long as possible. If you are open to moving to a facility, specify the type of facility you prefer, such as an assisted living community or a nursing home. Next, identify any specific care providers or agencies you trust. This can include particular home care agencies or facilities you have researched and found to have high standards of care. Lastly, consider your desired quality of life. This includes preferences for social activities, dietary needs, and other personal considerations contributing to your overall well-being. By documenting these preferences, you ensure that your care aligns with your values and enhances your quality of life.

Financial planning is a crucial component of long-term care planning. The costs associated with long-term care can be significant, making it essential to plan. Long-term care insurance is one option to consider. This type of insurance can help cover the costs of various care services, reducing the financial burden on you and your family. If you do not already have long-term care insurance, it might be worth exploring policies and their benefits. Savings and investments are another essential aspect. Setting aside funds specifically for long-term care can provide a financial cushion. Consider consulting with a financial advisor to create a plan that ensures you have the necessary funds when you need them. Government assistance programs, such as Medicaid, can also provide support. Understanding these programs' eligibility requirements and application process ensures you can access the benefits you are entitled to. By incorporating these financial strategies, you can manage the costs associated with long-term care more effectively.

Assessing your long-term care needs, exploring your options, documenting your preferences, and planning financially are all critical steps in preparing for the future. This comprehensive approach ensures you receive the care you need in your preferred setting without causing undue financial strain. By taking these steps, you provide clarity and peace of mind for yourself and your loved ones, ensuring that your long-term care aligns with your values and enhances your quality of life.

As we conclude this chapter on medical information and healthcare, remember that planning is about ensuring your well-being and making your wishes known. In the next chapter, we will delve into funeral and memorial planning, another crucial aspect of end-of-life preparation.

6

FUNERAL AND MEMORIAL WISHES

Planning your funeral arrangements not only ensures that your wishes are honored but also alleviates the burden on your loved ones during an emotional time. This chapter will guide you through the options and considerations between burial and cremation.

6.1 CHOOSING BURIAL OR CREMATION

Choosing between burial and cremation is a profoundly personal decision influenced by various factors, including religious beliefs, cultural traditions, financial considerations, and personal preferences. Understanding the options available can help you make an informed choice that reflects your values and wishes.

Traditional burial is perhaps the most familiar option. It involves placing the body in a casket and burying it in a cemetery. This method often includes a wake, a funeral, and a graveside ceremony. Traditional burial provides a physical place for loved ones to visit and pay their respects. However, it can be costly, including the casket, burial plot, headstone, and cemetery fees. Additionally, traditional burials have a significant environmental impact, requiring land and resources.

Green burial is an eco-friendly alternative that is gaining popularity. It aims to minimize the environmental impact by using biodegradable materials for the casket or shroud and avoiding embalming chemicals. The body is buried in a natural setting, such as a woodland or meadow, allowing it to decompose naturally and return to the earth. Green burials often cost less than traditional burials and can be a meaningful choice for those concerned about sustainability and environmental stewardship.

Cremation offers another option and has become increasingly popular. The process involves reducing the body to ashes using high heat. Cremation is more cost-effective than traditional burial, as it eliminates the need for a burial plot, casket, and headstone. According to the National Funeral Directors Association, cremation costs range from $2,000 to $3,000 through a funeral home and $1,500 to $3,000 for direct cremation through a crematory. The ashes can be kept in an urn, scattered in a meaningful location, or even incorporated into keepsakes like jewelry. Cremation provides flexibility in planning memorial services and can be more environmentally friendly, as it requires no land or space.

Alkaline hydrolysis, or "water cremation," is a newer, eco-friendly alternative to traditional cremation. This process uses a water-based solution and heat to break down the body, leaving behind a sterile liquid and bone fragments. Alkaline hydrolysis has a lower environmental impact than traditional cremation, producing fewer greenhouse gases and requiring less energy. It is gaining acceptance in some states and can be a thoughtful choice for those seeking an environmentally conscious option.

Religious and cultural beliefs often play a significant role in determining funeral preferences. For example, traditional burial is common in Christianity, but cremation is widely accepted among many denominations. In Judaism, Orthodox Jews typically oppose cremation, while Reform Jews are more accepting of it. In Islam, cremation is strictly forbidden, and burial is the only acceptable method. Hindus, on the other hand, traditionally practice cremation, except for babies, children, and saints. Understanding and respecting these religious and cultural practices can guide you in making a choice that aligns with your beliefs and values.

Evaluating the costs associated with each option is crucial for making an informed decision. Traditional burial tends to be the most expensive, with costs ranging from $10,000 to $12,000, including the casket, burial plot, headstone, and cemetery fees. Cremation is generally more affordable, with prices ranging from $2,000 to $3,000, and direct cremation being the most cost-effective option at $700 to $3,500. Green burials often fall somewhere between, depending on the materials used and the location. Alkaline hydrolysis costs can vary but are generally comparable to traditional cremation. Considering your budget and financial situation can help you choose a meaningful and affordable option.

Documenting your chosen method and any specific preferences ensures your wishes are honored. Specify the cemetery and any chosen plot if you prefer a traditional burial. If cremation is your choice, detail how you would like your ashes handled, whether kept in an urn, scattered in a specific location, or incorporated into keepsakes. For a green burial, indicate the natural burial site and any eco-friendly materials to be used. If you opt for alkaline hydrolysis, provide clear instructions on the process and how the remains should be handled. Including these details in your end-of-life planner and discussing them with your family ensures that your preferences are understood and respected.

As you consider your options, take the time to reflect on what matters most to you. Your choice of burial or cremation is a deeply personal decision that should align with your values, beliefs, and wishes. By documenting and communicating your preferences, you provide clarity and comfort to your loved ones, allowing them to honor your memory in a way that reflects your life and legacy.

6.2 DETAILED FUNERAL SERVICE PLANS

Planning your funeral service's structure can bring peace and fulfillment, knowing that your final goodbye will reflect your life and values. Start with the opening remarks, which set the tone for the entire service. These can be delivered by the officiant or a close family member, offering a warm welcome and a brief overview of what will follow. Readings and eulogies follow this. These segments allow friends and family to share personal stories, memories, and reflections. Choose individuals who know you well and can speak from the heart, providing comfort and connection to those gathered.

Music and hymns are another vital part of the service, offering emotional resonance and a chance for collective reflection. Select pieces that are special to you or your family. Music can evoke deep emotions and memories, whether a hymn sung during childhood church visits or a favorite song that always brings a smile. Closing remarks can get the service to a gentle and comforting conclusion. This is an opportunity for the officiant or another speaker to summarize the themes of the service, offer final words of comfort, and share a prayer or blessing.

Including personal touches in your funeral service ensures that it truly reflects who you are. Favorite songs or hymns can provide a musical backdrop that resonates with your life and personality. Personal anecdotes or stories shared during the eulogies can bring your character and experiences to life, offering a glimpse into the moments that defined you. Special readings or poems, chosen for their significance or emotional resonance, can add depth and meaning to the service. These elements create a more intimate and personalized experience, helping attendees feel connected to you and each other.

Designating participants for your service is essential to ensure that it runs smoothly and that your wishes are honored. Decide who you would like to serve as the officiant or religious leader, guiding the service and offering spiritual support. Choose eulogists and readers who can share meaningful stories and reflections, as their words will provide comfort and connection to those gathered. If you have musicians or soloists in mind, specify who they are and what pieces they should perform. Clear instructions and thoughtful choices make the service more meaningful and cohesive.

Planning for logistics and coordination is essential to ensure the service runs smoothly and meets your expectations. Selecting the right venue is a crucial first step. Consider a location that holds special significance to you, whether it's a place of worship, a community hall, or an outdoor setting. Consider seating arrangements to ensure all attendees are comfortable and can easily see and hear the proceedings. Organizing transportation for guests, especially those with difficulty traveling, ensures that everyone who wants to attend can do so. Though often overlooked, these practical arrangements play a significant role in creating a seamless and meaningful service.

Checklist for Funeral Service Plans:

- Outline the Service Structure:
- Opening remarks
- Readings and eulogies
- Music and hymns
- Closing remarks
- Include Personal Touches:
- Favorite songs or hymns
- Personal anecdotes or stories
- Special readings or poems
- Designate Participants:
- Officiant or religious leader
- Eulogists and readers
- Musicians or soloists
- Plan for Logistics and Coordination:
- Venue selection
- Seating arrangements

- Transportation for guests

This checklist can serve as a guide to ensure that your funeral service is thoughtfully planned and executed, reflecting your life and values in every detail. Take the time to consider each element and make choices that resonate with who you are and what you want your final farewell to convey. Your careful planning will provide comfort and clarity to your loved ones, allowing them to celebrate your life meaningfully and heartfeltly.

6.3 PRE-ARRANGED FUNERAL PLANS

Pre-arranged funeral plans offer significant advantages that can bring peace of mind to you and your family. One of the main benefits is reducing stress for your loved ones during an already emotional and challenging time. By making decisions in advance, you take the burden off your family, allowing them to focus on grieving and supporting each other. These plans ensure your wishes are honored, eliminating any guesswork for your family. Knowing that you have specified your preferences for everything from the type of service to the choice of music provides a sense of control and clarity. Additionally, pre-arranged plans can help with financial planning and cost control. Locking in prices at today's rates protects your family from future price increases and unexpected expenses.

Setting up pre-arranged funeral plans involves several steps designed to document and respect your wishes. The first step is meeting with a funeral director, who can guide you through the options and help you make informed decisions. During this meeting, you will discuss various services and merchandise, such as caskets, urns, and memorial keepsakes. The funeral director will provide information on different packages and customization options, allowing you to tailor the arrangements to your preferences. Once you have selected the services and merchandise, the next step is finalizing and documenting the arrangements. This involves signing a contract outlining your pre-arranged plan's details, ensuring everything is clearly specified and legally binding.

Funding pre-arranged funeral plans is another important consideration. Several options are available to ensure the financial aspects are handled in advance. Pre-payment plans allow you to pay for the funeral services over time, typically in monthly installments. This can make the financial burden more manageable and ensure the costs are covered when the time comes. Another option is funeral insurance, explicitly designed to cover funeral expenses. Funeral insurance policies can be tailored to your needs, providing a lump sum payment to your designated beneficiary upon passing. Trusts are also a viable option for funding pre-arranged plans. Setting up a trust allows you to allocate funds for your funeral expenses, ensuring the money is available when needed. Each option offers different benefits, and discussing them with a financial advisor can help you choose the best approach.

Communicating your pre-arranged plans to your family is crucial. Sharing the details with your next of kin ensures they know your wishes and where to find the necessary documents. It is essential to store contracts and receipts in a safe and accessible location, such as a fireproof safe or a secure drawer. Informing your family about the location of these documents prevents any confusion or delays when the time comes. Additionally, consider the legal aspects of pre-arranged plans. Updating your will to reflect your pre-arranged plans can clarify and ensure your wishes are legally recognized. Including specific instructions about the pre-arranged plans in your will helps avoid potential disputes or misunderstandings.

Making pre-arranged funeral plans involves thoughtful decision-making, financial planning, and clear communication with your loved ones. These steps ensure your final wishes are respected, and your family is spared from unnecessary stress and economic burden. The peace of mind that comes with knowing everything is taken care of is invaluable, allowing you to focus on living your life to the fullest.

6.4 WRITING YOUR OBITUARY

Writing your obituary might seem daunting, but it is essential in end-of-life planning. An obituary celebrates your life and achievements, providing a lasting tribute to family and friends. It offers a way to highlight the milestones that define your journey, from career accomplishments to personal passions. More than just a summary, an obituary provides closure for your loved ones, helping them grieve and remember you with fondness and respect. By crafting your obituary, you ensure your story is told how you want it to be, capturing the essence of who you are.

When writing your obituary, it's crucial to include several key components. Start with biographical information such as your full name, date, and place of birth. This establishes your identity and roots. Next, list your family and survivors. This includes parents, siblings, spouses, children, and grandchildren. Mentioning close family members recognizes their importance in your life and provides a sense of connection for those reading. Career and accomplishments should be highlighted to reflect your professional journey and the impact you made in your field. Whether you were a dedicated teacher, a skilled craftsman, or a successful business owner, these details add depth to your story.

Your hobbies and interests are another essential element to include. This is where you can share your passions, whether gardening, playing the piano, or volunteering at the local animal shelter. These personal touches give readers a glimpse into what brought you joy and fulfillment. They round out the portrait of your life, making it more relatable and memorable. By incorporating these aspects, your obituary becomes a comprehensive narrative that honors your legacy and comforts those left behind.

Crafting a meaningful obituary requires a respectful and uplifting tone. While it's important to acknowledge the loss, the focus should be on celebrating your life and achievements. Keep the language positive and inspirational, highlighting the good times and your impact on others. Including anecdotes and personal stories can make the obituary more engaging. Perhaps there's a funny story from a family vacation or a touching moment shared with a grandchild. These snippets of life add color and personality, making your obituary stand out. Reviewing and editing for accuracy is crucial. Ensure that all names, dates, and facts are correct. Having a trusted family member or friend read through the obituary for errors or omissions is a good idea.

Deciding where and how to publish your obituary is the final step. Local newspapers are a traditional choice and provide a way for the community to learn about your passing and pay their respects. Most newspapers have guidelines and templates to help you get started. Online memorial websites are another option. They offer a digital space where friends and family can leave messages, share photos, and celebrate your life. These platforms provide a lasting tribute that can be accessed anywhere in the world. Social media platforms like Facebook can also be used to share the obituary. This allows for a wider reach and enables friends and distant relatives to stay informed and offer condolences.

Writing your obituary ensures that your life is celebrated as you envision. It offers a lasting tribute highlighting your achievements, honors your relationships, and shares your passions. You create a comprehensive narrative that reflects who you are by including biographical information, family details, career accomplishments, and personal interests. Using a respectful and uplifting tone, incorporating anecdotes, and verifying accuracy ensures that your obituary is meaningful and memorable. Finally, choosing the appropriate platforms for publication allows your story to reach and resonate with those who knew and loved you.

6.5 MEMORIAL SERVICE PREFERENCES

Understanding the differences between a memorial service and a traditional funeral can help you decide the most fitting. A conventional funeral often occurs shortly after death and includes the presence of the body. In contrast, a memorial service offers more flexibility in timing and location since the body is not typically present. This flexibility allows for more thoughtful planning and can accommodate family members traveling from afar. Memorial services focus on celebrating life rather than mourning loss. They provide a platform for sharing stories, memories, and achievements, creating an atmosphere of remembrance and joy.

Personalizing your memorial service ensures it reflects your unique life and personality. Consider incorporating themed decorations that represent your interests and passions. For example, if you love gardening, decorate the venue with flowers and plants. Interactive elements like memory tables or video montages can be meaningful additions. A memory table can display cherished photos, keepsakes, and mementos that tell the story of your life. Video montages compile favorite moments, creating a visual narrative that resonates with attendees. These personal touches make the service more intimate and engaging, allowing your loved ones to connect with your memory deeply.

Designating roles for the memorial service is another crucial step. Choose a master of ceremonies to guide the event, ensuring it flows smoothly. This person should be someone who knows you well and can articulate your wishes with clarity and respect. Selecting speakers and storytellers is also essential. These individuals will share anecdotes, memories, and reflections, providing a personal touch to the service. Consider including performers if you wish to have music or readings. Whether it's a grandchild playing a favorite song on the piano or a friend reciting a beloved poem, these performances add emotional depth to the service.

Planning for memorial contributions instead of flowers can be a thoughtful gesture. Select charities or causes that are meaningful to you. Communicate these preferences to attendees through the memorial service announcement, ensuring they know how to contribute. Managing and acknowledging donations is essential.

Keep a record of contributors and send thank-you notes to express gratitude. This not only honors your memory but also supports causes that were important to you. It transforms the memorial service into an opportunity for a positive impact, extending your legacy beyond the event.

A memorial service offers a unique opportunity to celebrate your life authentically and meaningfully. By understanding the differences between a traditional funeral, personalizing the service, designating roles, and planning for contributions, you can create an event that honors your memory and comforts your loved ones.

6.6 SELECTING A FUNERAL HOME

Finding the proper funeral home is crucial in ensuring that your final wishes are made with dignity and respect. To begin, research funeral homes in your area. Online reviews and ratings can provide valuable insights into the experiences of others. Websites like Yelp and Google Reviews often include detailed feedback on the quality of services, professionalism, and overall satisfaction. Pay attention to positive and negative reviews, looking for patterns that indicate consistent strengths or weaknesses.

Additionally, recommendations from family and friends can be invaluable. Those who have gone through the process can offer first-hand accounts and suggest reputable funeral homes. Visiting and touring facilities is another crucial step. Seeing the premises in person allows you to gauge the atmosphere, cleanliness, and overall environment. It also allows you to meet the staff and ask questions, ensuring that you feel comfortable and confident in their ability to handle your arrangements.

When meeting with funeral directors, asking the right questions is essential to make an informed decision. Start by inquiring about the services offered. Different funeral homes may provide various options, from traditional funerals and cremations to green burials and memorial services. Understanding what is available can help you choose a funeral home that aligns with your preferences. Next, discuss pricing and payment options. Funeral costs vary significantly, so getting a clear breakdown of fees for essential, optional, and merchandise is vital. Ask about any available payment plans or financial assistance programs.

Additionally, it's essential to understand the funeral home's experience with specific religious or cultural practices. If you want to be honored with particular traditions or customs, ensure the funeral home has the knowledge and experience to accommodate these needs. This can include everything from specific rituals and ceremonies to dietary requirements for memorial receptions.

Comparing the services and packages offered by different funeral homes can help you make a well-informed choice. Basic service fees typically cover essential services such as body transportation, preparation, and filing necessary paperwork. However, optional services and merchandise can add to the overall cost. These might include embalming, cosmetology, and the use of a hearse or limousine. Some funeral homes offer customization options that allow you to tailor the arrangements to your specific wishes. This can include personalized caskets or urns, custom floral arrangements, and unique memorial keepsakes. By comparing these options, you can find a funeral home that provides the services and personalization you desire at a price that fits your budget.

Once you have selected a funeral home, it's essential to document your choice and communicate it to your family. Start by including the details in your end-of-life planner. This should encompass the name and contact information of the funeral home, a summary of the services and packages you have chosen, and any specific instructions or preferences. Inform your family members about your decision, ensuring they know which funeral home to contact and where to find the necessary documents. Storing contracts and agreements in a safe and accessible place, such as a fireproof safe or a secure drawer, is also crucial. This ensures your family can easily access the information when needed, preventing delays or confusion.

Selecting a funeral home involves careful research, asking the right questions, comparing services and packages, and documenting your choice. By taking these steps, you ensure that your final arrangements are handled with care and respect, reflecting your wishes and easing the burden on your loved ones. With this important decision, you are one step closer to completing your end-of-life planning.

7
PERSONAL LETTERS AND MESSAGES

Writing letters to your family members can give them emotional closure, a personal touch in communication, and tangible keepsakes they can cherish forever.

7.1 WRITING LETTERS TO FAMILY MEMBERS

Writing letters to your family is a significant way to express love and leave behind a piece of yourself. These letters can provide emotional closure for your loved ones, helping them navigate their grief and find comfort in your words. They can feel your presence and hear your voice when they read your letters, even when you are no longer there. The personal touch of a handwritten letter is irreplaceable; it shows that you took the time to put your thoughts and feelings into words. These letters become tangible keepsakes your family can hold onto, read, and re-read whenever they need to feel close to you.

Consider using a structured format to help you organize your thoughts and ensure your letters are comprehensive and heartfelt. Start with a warm greeting and introduction to set the tone for the letter. For instance, you might begin with, "Dear [Name], I hope this letter finds you well." This opening creates a sense of intimacy and connection. Next, share personal memories that you cherish. Reflect on special moments you have shared, lessons learned, and experiences shaping your relationship. This section allows you to celebrate your bond with each family member. Following this, express your gratitude and love. Let them know how much they mean to you and how grateful you are for their presence in your life. End with a closing and final thoughts, offering words of encouragement, wisdom, or simply a heartfelt goodbye.

Authenticity and honesty are essential when writing these letters. Use your voice and style to ensure that your personality shines through. Share personal anecdotes and stories that illustrate your feelings and experiences. Address any unresolved issues or feelings openly and with compassion. For example, you might write, "I remember when we had that disagreement, and I want you to know that I always valued our relationship, despite our differences." Being genuine and honest in your letters can provide a sense of resolution and peace for you and your loved ones.

Here are a few examples and prompts for writing your letters to inspire and get you started. You might begin with, "Dear [Name], I remember when we..." and share a cherished memory. This could be a family vacation, a milestone celebration, or a simple everyday moment with special meaning. Another prompt could be, "I am so grateful for the times we shared..." to express your gratitude for the moments and experiences you have had together. Finally, you could write, "I want you to know how much you mean to me..." to convey your deep affection and appreciation for your loved one. These prompts can help you find the right words and ensure your letters are heartfelt and meaningful.

Consider creating a space in your planner to jot down thoughts and memories as they come to you. This can be a dedicated section where you can draft your letters, refine your words, and ensure that each letter captures the essence of your relationship with each family member. Remember, the goal is to leave behind a piece of yourself that your loved ones can hold onto and cherish forever. Writing these letters may be an emotional process, but it is also an opportunity to reflect on the love and connections that have enriched your life.

Reflection Section: Drafting Your First Letter

Take a moment to reflect on a special memory you share with a family member. Write a few sentences about this memory, capturing the emotions and significance of the moment. Next, express gratitude for this memory and its impact on your relationship. Finally, offer a few words of love and encouragement. Use this reflection as a starting point for your letter, and let your thoughts flow naturally from there.

Writing letters to your family members is a lasting gift that they will treasure. Your words can provide comfort, evoke memories, and keep your spirit alive in their hearts.

7.2 CRAFTING MESSAGES FOR FRIENDS

The unique bond you share with your friends is something extraordinary. Friends are the family we choose for ourselves; the memories and experiences you have shared with them are priceless. Leaving messages for your close friends acknowledges this special bond and celebrates the moments you've spent together. It's a way to thank them for their companionship and support and to let them know how much they have meant to you. These messages can be a source of comfort and joy, reminding them of the times you've laughed, cried, and grown together.

To help you craft these heartfelt messages, consider using a structured format that ensures you cover all the essential aspects of your friendship. Start with an opening greeting that sets a warm and personal tone. For example, "Dear [Name], I've been thinking about all the wonderful times we've shared." This immediately creates a connection and draws your friend into the message. Next, recount shared experiences that have defined your friendship. Reflect on the adventures, challenges, and milestones you've experienced together. This could be anything from a memorable trip to a simple yet meaningful everyday moment. Sharing these memories will bring a smile to your friend's face and reinforce the strength of your bond.

After reminiscing about shared experiences, move on to expressing your appreciation and affection. Tell your friend how much you value their friendship and its meaning. You might say, "I always admired your ability to make me laugh, even on the toughest days," or "Thank you for being there when I needed someone to talk to." These expressions of gratitude will touch your friend's heart and remind them of their impact on your life. Finally, conclude with final words and wishes. Offer your friend encouragement, share your hopes for their future, and let them know that they will always hold a special place in your heart.

Specificity and personalization are critical when crafting these messages. Mention particular events or milestones that have been significant in your friendship. Highlight the qualities and traits you admire in your friend, such as their kindness, resilience, or sense of humor. This makes the message more meaningful and shows that you truly know and appreciate them. For example, you might write, "Remember the trip we took to the mountains? I'll never forget how we got lost but ended up having the best time exploring new paths." Or, "I always admired your ability to stay calm under pressure; it's something I've tried to emulate in my own life."

To inspire you further, here are some sample messages and prompts to guide your writing. You could start with, "Remember the trip we took to..." and recount a particularly memorable adventure. This could be a road trip, a vacation, or even a spontaneous outing that turned into an unforgettable experience. Another prompt could be, "I always admired your ability to..." to highlight a trait or quality you respect in your friend. This could be their patience, creativity, or unwavering support. Finally, you might write, "Thank you for being there when..." to express gratitude for their presence during significant moments. This could be during a personal crisis, an important achievement, or when you need a friend.

Sample Message Example

"Dear Jane, I've been thinking about all the wonderful times we've shared. Remember the trip we took to the beach last summer? I'll never forget how we stayed up all night talking and watching the sunrise. You've always had a way of making even the simplest moments feel special. I always admired your ability to listen without judgment and offer support when I needed it most. Thank you for being there when I needed someone to talk to after my surgery. Your friendship has been a constant source of strength and joy in my life. I wish you all the happiness in the world and hope that we will always stay connected. With love, Mary."

Crafting these messages for your friends allows you to leave behind a piece of your heart and soul. Your words will serve as a lasting testament to your bond, bringing comfort and joy to your friends whenever they read them.

7.3 CREATING A VIDEO MESSAGE

Creating a video message adds a personal and dynamic touch to your farewells. Unlike written words, video messages allow you to use visual and auditory elements to convey your message. Your expressions, tone of voice, and even the way you pause can communicate emotions that words alone might miss. These elements capture your personality and make your message more impactful. A video message creates a lasting digital keepsake that your loved ones can watch whenever they need to feel close to you. It's an opportunity to speak directly to them, share your thoughts, and leave a piece of yourself that they can revisit.

Choosing the right location and lighting is crucial when recording a video message. Find a quiet, well-lit space where you won't be interrupted. Natural light is ideal, so try to sit near a window, but avoid direct sunlight that can cause harsh shadows. If natural light is unavailable, use a lamp to illuminate your face evenly. Make sure the background is free of distractions. Using a reliable recording device is also essential. Most smartphones and tablets have good cameras, but if you can access a higher-quality camera, use it. Ensure clear audio by minimizing background noise and speaking directly into the microphone. If possible, use an external microphone to enhance sound quality.

Content and structure are critical to a meaningful video message. Start with a brief introduction, stating the purpose of your message. For example, you might say, "Hi, everyone. I wanted to leave this message to share some of my favorite memories and express my love for you all." This sets the stage for what's to come. Move on to sharing personal stories and memories. Talk about experiences that have shaped your relationships and moments that you cherish. This part of the message will evoke emotions and bring your loved ones closer to you. Next, express your love and gratitude. Tell them how much they mean to you and how grateful you are for their support and companionship. Finally, offer your final words and wishes. This could include encouragement, advice, or simply a heartfelt goodbye.

Being natural and at ease in front of the camera will make your message more authentic and impactful. Practicing beforehand can help you feel more comfortable. You should jot down key points you want to cover, but avoid reading from a script. Speak from the heart and let your emotions guide you. Keeping the message concise and focused will ensure that your words have the most impact. Remember, it's not about perfection; it's about authenticity. Your loved ones will appreciate your effort and cherish your message, no matter how polished.

Practical Tips for Recording High-Quality Videos

Keep the camera at eye level or slightly above when recording your video message. This framing ensures that you are captured from the top of your head to the top of your chest, leaving a little space at the top of the frame. Ensure the CAMERA icon is on to confirm the video is active. If you experience frequent freezing, turn off the

CAMERA to save bandwidth. Avoid standing before a window to prevent backlighting; use a lamp to light your face and soften the light with a sheer cloth if needed. Record using a computer or smartphone camera for crisper quality. Ensure you're in a quiet room with doors shut to eliminate noise. Add fabric to rooms with hard surfaces to soften sound. Confirm the MIC icon is on and not muted when speaking. Speak, look directly into the camera, and avoid excessive movement. Avoid shuffling papers or making small movements that create noise. Ensure a strong internet connection to avoid interruptions.

Ultimately, creating a video message is a powerful way to leave a lasting legacy. By combining visual and auditory elements, you can convey emotions and thoughts in a way that written words might not fully capture. Your loved ones will treasure this digital keepsake, and it will provide them with comfort and connection in the years to come.

7.4 SHARING WISDOM AND LIFE LESSONS

Imparting wisdom and life lessons can be one of the most meaningful legacies you leave behind. By passing on your experiences and insights, you guide future generations, providing them with the tools and perspectives they might need to navigate life's challenges. Your wisdom can offer comfort and inspiration as a beacon during difficult times. For example, sharing how you overcame adversity or the values that guided you can profoundly impact your loved ones. These lessons can help them make informed decisions and find strength when facing trials.

Organizing your thoughts and themes can make this process more manageable and impactful. Start by categorizing your lessons into love, perseverance, and integrity themes. This thematic approach helps structure your wisdom, making it easier for the reader to absorb and reflect on each lesson. Use anecdotes to illustrate your points; stories from your life can make abstract lessons more concrete and relatable. For instance, if you want to impart the value of perseverance, recount a time when you faced a significant obstacle and how you overcame it. Keep your messages concise and focused, ensuring each lesson is clear and straightforward. This approach prevents your wisdom from becoming overwhelming and keeps the reader engaged.

Reflective writing is crucial when sharing life lessons. Take your time to think deeply about the experiences and insights you want to convey. Journaling exercises can be beneficial in gathering your thoughts. Spend a few minutes each day writing about different aspects of your life, focusing on the lessons you've learned. Revisit your drafts to ensure your messages are as clear and impactful as possible. This process of reflection and revision helps distill your wisdom into its most essential form, making it more powerful and meaningful for the reader.

Here are some examples and prompts for writing your wisdom messages to get you started. You might begin with, "One important lesson I learned is..." and share a significant insight from your life. This could be anything from kindness's importance to hard work's value. Another prompt could be, "In difficult times, remember to..." offering advice on navigating challenges. This could include strategies for staying resilient, maintaining hope, or relying on loved ones for support. Finally, you might write, "Always value..." to highlight the principles and values that have guided you. This could be honesty, compassion, or the importance of family.

Reflection Section: Drafting Your Wisdom Messages

Take a few minutes to reflect on a significant lesson you've learned. Please write down the critical points of this lesson, including any stories or experiences that illustrate it. Next, consider how this lesson can benefit your loved ones and write a few sentences explaining its importance. Use this reflection as the basis for your wisdom message, ensuring it is clear, concise, and impactful.

By sharing your wisdom and life lessons, you provide a lasting legacy that can guide and inspire future generations. Your experiences and insights are valuable, and taking the time to document them ensures that your loved ones can benefit from your knowledge long after you're gone. This sharing can bring comfort and strength to your family, helping them navigate their lives with the wisdom you've imparted.

7.5 PERSONALIZING FAREWELL NOTES

Personalizing farewell notes makes them more meaningful because they reflect your unique relationships with each recipient. When you add specific touches that only you and the other person understand, you take the time to think about them individually. This level of detail makes the note feel exceptional and genuine. It's not just a generic farewell; it's a heartfelt message tailored to the person you're addressing. For example, mentioning a shared inside joke or a nickname can evoke memories and feelings that a more general note cannot.

To tailor your notes effectively, consider using nicknames or pet names that you have for the person. These terms of endearment add a layer of intimacy and show that the note is meant just for them. Mention specific memories that you have shared. For instance, if you and a friend always went fishing every summer, recalling a particularly memorable trip can make the note come alive. Also, highlight personal traits or qualities that you admire in the recipient. If your sister has always been the family's peacemaker, acknowledging this can make her feel valued and recognized. This specificity ensures that your message resonates on a deeper level.

Encouraging creativity and expression in your notes can enhance their impact. Handwritten notes provide a personal touch that typed messages lack. Putting pen to paper can make your words feel more genuine. Adding drawings or decorations can also make the note more visually appealing. Even simple sketches or embellishments can add character and charm. Using unique stationery or paper can elevate the experience of reading the note, making it feel like a cherished keepsake. These creative elements show that you put effort and thought into your farewell, making it even more meaningful.

Here are some examples and prompts for your personalized farewell notes to get you started. You might begin with, "Dear [Name], you always made me smile when..." and follow up with a specific instance that captures the essence of your relationship. For example, "Dear John, you always made me smile when we went hiking and you'd make up silly songs about the trails." Another prompt could be, "I will never forget the time we..." which allows you to recount a significant experience you shared. For instance, "I will never forget the time we got lost in the city but ended up discovering that amazing little café." Finally, you might write, "You have a special place in my heart because..." to express the unique qualities that make the person important to you. An example could be, "You have a special place in my heart because you always know how to make everyone feel at home."

Personalizing your farewell notes creates a lasting impression that the recipient can treasure. Your words will provide comfort and joy as a tangible reminder of your bond. These notes are more than just farewells; they are tokens of your relationship, filled with memories and emotions that transcend time.

Checklist: Personalizing Farewell Notes

- Use nicknames or pet names for a personal touch.
- Mention specific memories or inside jokes.
- Highlight the recipient's traits or qualities.
- Handwrite your notes for added sincerity.
- Add drawings or decorations to enhance visual appeal.
- Use unique stationery or paper to make the note feel like a keepsake.

Personalizing your farewell notes is a meaningful way to show your love and appreciation for the people in your life. Your unique touches make each note special, creating a lasting memory that will be cherished.

7.6 STORING AND PRESENTING YOUR MESSAGES

Storing your personal letters, messages, and video recordings securely is crucial. These heartfelt messages are precious; you want to preserve them for your loved ones. Losing such invaluable pieces can be devastating, so proper storage is essential. Keeping your messages safe prevents loss or damage and ensures they are easily accessible when your family needs them the most.

For written messages, physical storage options include using envelopes or boxes. You can store each letter in envelopes labeled with the recipient's name and the date. These envelopes can then be placed in a sturdy box, which should be kept in a dry, cool place to prevent damage from moisture or heat. Acid-free paper and archival-quality boxes are ideal for preserving the integrity of your letters. For digital messages, consider using cloud services or USB drives. Cloud storage offers the advantage of being accessible from anywhere, while USB drives provide a tangible backup. Using both methods ensures redundancy; if one fails, the other remains available. Combining physical and digital storage offers an added layer of security, safeguarding your messages against unforeseen events.

Presenting your messages to your loved ones can be as thoughtful as writing them. Creating a memory box or binder is a beautiful way to organize and present your letters. A memory box can hold envelopes, small souvenirs, and even a flash drive with video messages. A binder allows you to organize letters by the recipient, making it easy for each family member to find their messages. Including instructions for when to open the messages adds a special touch. For example, you might write a note indicating that a particular letter should be opened on a significant date, such as a birthday or anniversary. This thoughtful planning ensures your messages are received at meaningful moments, providing comfort and connection when needed.

Updating and adding to your collection of messages is also important. Life is dynamic, and new events and experiences will continue to shape your relationships. Regularly reviewing and updating your messages keeps them relevant and reflective of your thoughts and feelings. Set aside time periodically to revisit your letters and video messages. Add new messages for significant events, such as the birth of a grandchild, a wedding, or other milestones. Keeping a log of stored messages helps you track your writing and ensures everything is noticed. This log can be a simple list indicating who each message is for and the date it was written, making it easier to manage and update your collection.

Call-to-Action: Organize Your Messages

Take a moment to gather all the letters, notes, and video messages you've created. Store them in a way that ensures they are safe and accessible. Consider a combination of physical and digital storage for added security. Periodically review and update your messages to keep them current. By organizing and preserving your heartfelt messages, you provide your loved ones with lasting keepsakes they can cherish for years.

Ending Chapter: By thoughtfully storing and presenting your messages, you ensure that your words of love, wisdom, and farewell remain safe and accessible. Your loved ones will treasure these messages, providing comfort and connection long after you're gone. As we move forward, we'll explore the final details and special instructions that will further ensure your wishes are honored and your legacy is preserved.

8

FINAL DETAILS AND SPECIAL INSTRUCTIONS

This chapter will guide you through how to provide for your pets in your end-of-life planning.

8.1 PET CARE INSTRUCTIONS

Detailing daily care routines for your pets is crucial to ensure they receive the same love and attention they are accustomed to. Start by specifying feeding schedules and portion sizes for each pet. For instance, if your dog eats twice daily, note the specific times and the amount of food given. Include details about any dietary restrictions or special treats. Exercise routines are equally important. If your cat enjoys a daily play session with a laser pointer or your dog needs a morning walk, make sure to document these activities. Favorite activities like a specific toy or game should also be noted to maintain their happiness. Grooming requirements should be clearly outlined, such as brushing schedules, bathing routines, and nail trimming. This ensures that whoever takes over their care understands how to keep them clean and healthy.

Veterinary care is another critical aspect of your pet's well-being.

Include comprehensive details about their veterinary clinic, such as the name, address, and contact information. Regular check-up schedules should be documented, including the frequency of visits and specific tests or procedures. For example, this should be noted if your cat requires a dental cleaning every six months. Document your pet's medical history, including past surgeries, illnesses, and current medications. List the dosage and frequency of each drug, along with any potential side effects to watch for. This information will help the new caretaker provide consistent and informed care.

Identifying caretakers is essential to ensure your pets are looked after by someone you trust. Specify the names and contact information of potential caretakers. It's wise to have a primary caretaker and one or two backup options if the primary caretaker is unavailable. For example, Alice chose her niece as the primary caretaker for her dogs and her neighbor for her cats. Written agreements or consent from these caretakers should be obtained to confirm their willingness to take on this responsibility. This ensures no misunderstandings or disputes about who will care for your pets. These agreements in writing provide peace of mind for you and the caretakers.

Providing financial provisions for pet care is essential to meet your pets' needs without burdening their new caretakers. Setting up a pet trust fund is an effective way to allocate funds for their care. According to the Werner Law Firm, a pet trust includes specific instructions for the pet's care and is funded by a portion of your estate. The trustee of a pet trust is bound by a fiduciary duty to care for the pet according to your instructions. Determine your pets' estimated monthly and annual expenses, including food, grooming, veterinary care, and other necessities. Provide clear instructions for accessing and managing these funds. For instance, you might allocate a certain monthly amount for food and grooming, with additional funds available for veterinary care. Designate a remainder beneficiary for unused funds, ensuring your wishes are fully honored.

Checklist: Pet Care Instructions

- Detail daily care routines, including feeding schedules, portion sizes, exercise routines, and grooming requirements.
- Include comprehensive veterinary information, such as clinic name, contact information, check-up schedules, and medical history.
- Identify caretakers by name, contact information, and written agreements or consent.
- Establish a pet trust fund, estimate monthly and annual expenses, and provide instructions for accessing and managing funds to offer financial provisions for pet care.

By taking these steps, you ensure your beloved pets will continue receiving the care and attention they deserve, even when you cannot provide it yourself.

8.2 LISTING EMERGENCY CONTACTS

When it comes to emergencies, having a well-organized list of contacts can be a lifesaver. Start by identifying key emergency contacts, including family members, close friends, and neighbors who can provide immediate assistance. For instance, your daughter, who lives nearby, might be the first person to call if something happens, while a close friend could help with smaller tasks like picking up groceries or medication. Remember to include neighbors who can quickly respond in an emergency at home. Additionally, list medical professionals and healthcare providers such as your primary care doctor, specialist, or any home healthcare aides you rely on regularly.

Each contact should include detailed information about their specific roles and responsibilities. Write down their full names, relationships to you, phone numbers, and email addresses. For example, your son might be listed as an executor, meaning he will handle legal and financial matters. At the same time, your spouse could be the healthcare proxy, making medical decisions on your behalf. Clarity is critical here; specify duties like who is responsible for your medical care decisions or who will manage your financial affairs. This ensures everyone knows their role and can act swiftly and appropriately when needed.

Organizing these contacts for quick access is crucial. A printed contact list can be kept in a prominent place, such as on the refrigerator or near the telephone. Digital storage options are also beneficial. You can store a list on your smartphone or use a cloud service for easy accessibility. Make sure your family members know where to find this information. You might also consider using a combination of both printed and digital lists to ensure redundancy. The goal is to make sure that in an emergency, the contact information is easily accessible to anyone who needs it.

It's essential to update this contact information regularly to keep it current. Set reminders to review and update the list periodically. Do this annually or after significant life events like moving, changes in health, or relationships. Notify your contacts when their information is included so they know their roles. Regularly reviewing and revising contact roles ensures the list remains accurate and useful. For example, if your neighbor moves away, you must update your list with a new emergency contact who lives nearby.

Checklist: Emergency Contact List

- Identify key emergency contacts, including family, friends, neighbors, and medical professionals.
- Include full names, relationships, phone numbers, and email addresses.
- Specify roles and responsibilities, such as executor or healthcare proxy.
- Create a printed contact list and consider digital storage options.
- Ensure the list is easily accessible to family members.

- Regularly update contact information and notify contacts of their roles.
- Review and revise contact roles as needed.

8.3 ORGANIZING IMPORTANT DOCUMENTS AND LOCATIONS

Creating a comprehensive list of essential documents is the first step in ensuring everything is in order and easily accessible. Start with legal documents like your will, power of attorney, and advance directives. These documents outline your wishes and designate who will decide on your behalf. Next, compile all financial records, including bank statements, investment portfolios, and retirement account information. These records provide a complete picture of your financial situation and are essential for managing your estate. Remember medical records, including insurance policies, medical history, and prescriptions. Having all this information in one place can save time and reduce stress for your loved ones.

Specifying the locations of these critical items is equally important. Physical storage locations like a safe or filing cabinet are common choices. Ensure these locations are secure yet accessible to trusted individuals. Digital storage options, such as encrypted cloud services or USB drives, offer additional security and convenience—clearly document where each item is stored and how to access it. For instance, if your will is in a safe deposit box, note the bank's location and the box number. If your medical records are stored digitally, provide instructions on accessing the files, including any necessary passwords. This clarity helps ensure that your documents can be found quickly when needed.

Including backup copies of critical documents is an intelligent safeguard against loss or damage. Scanning and digitizing paper documents create electronic versions that can be easily stored and shared. Store these digital copies with trusted family members or your attorney to ensure they are accessible in an emergency. Regularly updating these backup copies is crucial to keep them current. Set a schedule to review and update your documents, perhaps annually or after significant life events. This practice ensures that all information remains accurate and up-to-date, providing peace of mind that your wishes will be followed.

Providing access instructions for executors and family members is the final piece of the puzzle. Ensure your executors and critical family members know how to access these documents. Share access codes or keys with them and provide written instructions for accessing digital files. This might include step-by-step guides on using encryption software or accessing cloud storage. Regularly reviewing access procedures with the involved parties ensures everyone is familiar with them and can act swiftly if needed. This preparation helps eliminate confusion and delays during critical times, making it easier for your loved ones to manage your affairs.

Checklist: Organizing Important Documents and Locations

- Create a comprehensive document list, including legal, financial, and medical records.
- Specify physical and digital storage locations, with instructions for access.
- Include backup copies by scanning and digitizing paper documents.
- Store copies with trusted family members or attorneys.
- Regularly update backup copies to keep information current.
- Provide access instructions for executors and family members.
- Share access codes or keys and written instructions for digital files.
- Regularly review access procedures with involved parties.

8.4 SPECIAL INSTRUCTIONS FOR PERSONAL BELONGINGS

When it comes to your personal belongings, specifying who gets what can alleviate potential conflicts and ensure that your cherished items go to those who will appreciate them most. Describe specific bequests for valuable items such as jewelry, art, and collectibles. Write down the description of each item, including any unique identifiers like serial numbers or certificates of authenticity. This level of detail ensures no confusion about which item goes to whom. For instance, if you have a diamond necklace that you want to pass on, describe it in detail, noting its cut, carat, and any unique features.

Sentimental items, such as family heirlooms and photo albums, often carry more emotional weight than monetary value. These items should also be documented in your bequests. Specify the intended recipient's name and include any special instructions for the transfer. For instance, you might want your grandmother's quilt to go to your eldest granddaughter, with a note explaining its history and significance. If the primary recipient is unavailable, provide an alternative. This ensures that your wishes are honored even if circumstances change. For example, if your granddaughter cannot take the quilt, specify that it should go to your niece.

Proper storage and maintenance of valuable and sentimental items are crucial for preserving their condition and ensuring future generations can enjoy them. Document the storage locations and conditions for these items. For instance, jewelry should be stored in a secure, dry place to prevent tarnishing. Art pieces might need climate-controlled conditions to avoid damage. Provide evident care and maintenance instructions. This might include cleaning and preserving the items and any professional services that might be necessary. For example, valuable paintings may require periodic cleaning by a professional conservator. Also, access instructions should be included for caretakers or recipients to ensure they can maintain these items properly.

Legal considerations are a vital aspect of transferring personal belongings. Include these items in your will or estate plan to bind the bequests legally. According to Nolo, an individual property memorandum can be helpful for this purpose. This document allows you to leave specific personal items to loved ones without updating your will, provided it is mentioned in the will to be legally binding. You can change the memorandum as often as you want without needing witnesses or a notary public. However, not all states recognize personal property memoranda, so it's essential to consult with an attorney to ensure your documents comply with state laws. For complex distributions, such as those involving high-value items or contentious family dynamics, professional legal guidance can help prevent disputes and ensure your wishes are followed.

Checklist: Special Instructions for Personal Belongings

- Detail-specific bequests for valuable items like jewelry, art, and collectibles, including descriptions and unique identifiers.
- Document sentimental items such as family heirlooms and photo albums, specifying the intended recipient and any special instructions for the transfer.
- Provide alternatives if the primary recipient is unavailable.
- Include details on storage locations, conditions for valuable items, and care and maintenance instructions.
- Provide access instructions for caretakers or recipients to ensure proper maintenance.
- Include personal belongings in your will or estate plan to bind bequests legally.
- Consider using a personal property memorandum for specific items, ensuring it is mentioned in your will.
- Consult with an attorney for complex distributions to prevent disputes and ensure compliance with state laws.

By documenting your wishes for personal belongings, you can ensure that these items are cherished and maintained by those who will appreciate them most. This preserves your legacy and provides your loved ones clarity and peace of mind.

8.5 REGULARLY UPDATING YOUR PLANNER

As life evolves, so should your end-of-life planner. Establishing a routine for regular reviews ensures that your documents remain current and relevant. An annual review of all sections is a practical approach. Set aside a specific time each year to thoroughly review your planner. Look at every aspect, from legal documents to personal messages. This helps catch any outdated information and allows you to make necessary adjustments. Major life events, such as marriage, the birth of a child, or a significant change in health, also warrant immediate updates. These events can substantially alter your plans, and it's crucial to reflect these changes promptly. Additionally, quarterly check-ins for financial and medical information should be considered. Financial markets can fluctuate, and your health status can change, making it essential to keep these sections up-to-date.

Documenting changes is another crucial step. Use different colors or markings to highlight updates, making them easily identifiable. This visual differentiation helps avoid confusion and ensures that anyone reviewing your planner understands what has been modified. Always include dates of revisions next to the changes. This practice provides a timeline of updates, showing the progression of your decisions and making it easier to track any modifications. Notifying relevant parties of significant changes is equally important. If you update your healthcare proxy or change the executor of your will, inform those involved. Clear communication ensures that everyone knows their responsibilities and can act accordingly.

Consistency across all documents is crucial for maintaining the integrity of your planner. Ensure that legal and financial records are updated simultaneously to reflect any changes accurately. Cross-referencing different sections for accuracy helps maintain coherence. For instance, if you update your will to include a new grandchild, ensure this addition is reflected in any trust documents or financial plans. This consistency allows for discrepancies that could lead to legal complications or misunderstandings. Keeping all documents aligned ensures that your wishes are unambiguous.

Involving family members in the update process can foster transparency and prevent future conflicts. Regular family meetings to review changes provide an opportunity for open discussions. This practice ensures that everyone understands your decisions and the reasons behind them. Sharing updated sections with executors and critical contacts is equally important. Please provide copies of the revised documents or inform them where to find the updated versions. This proactive approach keeps everyone on the same page and ensures your wishes are respected. By involving your loved ones, you create a support system that can help manage your affairs smoothly when the time comes.

8.6 ENSURING ACCESSIBILITY AND SECURITY

Balancing accessibility and security for your end-of-life planner is crucial. You want your loved ones to find and use your planner easily, but you must also protect it from unauthorized access. Start with secure physical storage. A locked safe is an excellent option for securing your documents yet accessible. Choose a fireproof and waterproof safe to protect against natural disasters. Place the safe in a discreet but reachable location within your home. Share the combination or key with trusted individuals only. Avoid labeling the safe too obviously; subtlety keeps it secure.

Encrypting digital copies of your planner adds another layer of security. Use reputable encryption software to protect your files. Store these encrypted copies on a USB drive or in a secure cloud service. Ensure that solid passwords back your digital storage options and, if possible, two-factor authentication. This makes it harder for unauthorized persons to access your files. Share access to these encrypted files with trusted individuals by providing them with the necessary passwords and instructions. Ensure they understand how to use the encryption software to access the documents. This balance of accessibility and security ensures your planner is protected and easy to access when needed.

Creating a plan for emergency access to your planner is essential. Designate specific emergency contacts with permission to access your planner during critical times. Provide these contacts with sealed instructions detailing how to access your planner. This might include the location of your safe and the combination of passwords for digital files. Ensure that these instructions are clear and concise. Store these sealed instructions where your emergency contacts can easily find them, such as with other essential documents they already have access to. This preparation ensures that your planner can be accessed swiftly and efficiently in an emergency without compromising security.

Addressing potential security risks is vital to maintaining your planner's integrity. Unauthorized access is a primary concern. Regularly change passwords and security codes associated with your digital files and physical storage to mitigate this risk. Use complex passwords that combine letters, numbers, and special characters. Identity theft is another significant risk. Safeguard against this by limiting the number of people who have access to your planner and by ensuring those who do are trustworthy. Be vigilant about who knows the location of your safe and the passwords to your digital files. Regularly review who has access and adjust as necessary to maintain security.

Regularly reviewing and updating your security measures is a proactive way to stay ahead of potential threats. Conduct annual security audits of both your physical and digital storage solutions. Check the integrity of your safe and update any worn-out components. Review your digital encryption methods and update them if better options become available. Updating encryption and access protocols ensures your methods remain robust against evolving security threats. Consulting with security professionals can provide expert advice tailored to your specific needs. They can offer insights into the latest security technologies and practices, helping you keep your planner secure.

By taking these steps, you can ensure that your end-of-life planner remains accessible to those who need it while being secure from unauthorized access. This careful balance provides peace of mind, knowing your plans are protected and can be executed smoothly when the time comes.

The next chapter will explore how to communicate your final wishes to your family and friends, ensuring everyone understands and respects your plans. This final step will help you tie everything together, completing your end-of-life planning.

CONCLUSION

End-of-life planning is crucial in providing peace of mind for you and your loved ones. Taking control of your final affairs ensures that your wishes are honored and your family is spared unnecessary stress and confusion during difficult times. This book aims to guide you through this process, making it manageable and transparent.

We've covered many topics, starting with the importance of end-of-life planning. We've discussed why overcoming emotional barriers and setting clear objectives is essential. We delved into the necessary legal documents, such as wills, power of attorney, and advance directives. We organized financial affairs, documented digital presence, and compiled comprehensive medical information. We planned for funerals and memorials, wrote personal letters, and ensured that special instructions were clear. Each chapter provided detailed guidance, practical examples, and actionable steps to help you navigate this journey.

The key takeaways from this book are straightforward but powerful. First, documenting your wishes reduces stress for your family. It prevents disputes and ensures that your intentions are clear. Second, legal preparedness protects your assets and ensures they are distributed according to your wishes. Third, organizing your financial and digital lives makes it easier for your loved ones to manage your affairs. Fourth, clear medical directives ensure that your healthcare preferences are honored, even when you cannot communicate them. Finally, personal letters and special instructions provide emotional closure and a personal touch, leaving a lasting legacy.

Now, it's time to take action. If you still need to start, begin by setting aside time to work on your end-of-life planner. Break it down into manageable tasks and set realistic deadlines. Gather the necessary documents, converse with your family, and consult with professionals. Remember, this process can be completed in stages. Consistent, small steps will lead to significant progress.

Thank you for taking this journey through such a necessary process. Your commitment to planning for the future demonstrates care and love for your family. By addressing these challenging topics, you are taking a significant step towards ensuring peace and clarity for everyone involved.

If you need further support or resources, many are available to help you. Legal aid organizations can assist with drafting documents and understanding legal requirements. Online platforms like PREPARE for Your Care and The Conversation Project offer tools and forms to help you draft your advance directives. Many state health departments provide free advance directive forms on their official websites. Organizations like AARP and the National Hospice and Palliative Care Organization offer comprehensive resources for end-of-life planning.

Thank you again for your dedication to this vital task. By completing your end-of-life planner, you are providing an invaluable gift to your loved ones. Your foresight and care will ensure your wishes are respected, and your family can focus on celebrating your life and legacy.

HAPPINESS BEGINS WITH ACTION

Congratulations on discovering the ways you can plan for the future. If you've started implementing the strategies you found in this book, you may already notice you feel more at ease and secure. I hope this book has helped you get there. If so, please share your thoughts with others who need to make a plan.

WANT TO HELP OTHERS?

Just scan the QR Code below:

BIBLIOGRAPHY

- *Making plans and decisions for the end of your life* https://www.betterhealth.vic.gov.au/health/servicesandsupport/making-plans-and-decisions-for-the-end-of-your-life
- *What happens if you die without a will?* https://www.legalzoom.com/articles/what-happens-if-you-die-without-a-will
- *Five Myths About Advance Care Planning* https://www.nia.nih.gov/health/advance-care-planning/five-myths-about-advance-care-planning
- *Palliative Care Patients Tell Their Stories* https://www.aha.org/center/palliative-care/patient-stories
- *Advance Care Planning: Advance Directives for Health Care* https://www.nia.nih.gov/health/advance-care-planning/advance-care-planning-advance-directives-health-care
- *State Requirements for Living Wills* https://www.rocketlawyer.com/family-and-personal/health-and-medical/healthcare-decisions/legal-guide/state-requirements-for-living-wills
- *Power of Attorney (POA): Meaning, Types, and How and Why ...* https://www.investopedia.com/terms/p/powerofattorney.asp
- *How to Revoke or Override a Power of Attorney Form* https://bluenotary.us/how-to-override-or-revoke-a-power-of-attorney/
- *Estate Planning Guide and Checklist for 2024* https://www.ncoa.org/adviser/estate-planning/estate-planning-guide-checklist/
- *Accounting and Reporting – 8 Best Practices for Investment ...* https://www.pkfod.com/wp-content/uploads/2019/03/Accounting-and-Reporting-%E2%80%93-8-Best-Practices-for-Investment-Advisors-FINAL.pdf
- *Debts and Deceased Relatives | Consumer Advice* https://consumer.ftc.gov/articles/debts-and-deceased-relatives
- *The Role of Life Insurance in Estate Planning* https://www.tbhr-law.com/the-role-of-life-insurance-in-estate-planning
- *Free Password Templates and Spreadsheets* https://www.smartsheet.com/free-password-templates
- *Appoint a Digital Executor in Your Estate Plan* https://www.rocketlawyer.com/family-and-personal/estate-planning/make-a-will/legal-guide/appoint-digital-executor-estate-plan
- *The Best Password Managers for 2024* https://www.pcmag.com/picks/the-best-password-managers

- *Set up Your Inactive Account Manager - Guidebooks - Google* https://guidebooks.google.com/online-security/protect-your-google-account/inactive-account-manager?hl=en-us#:~:text=To%20-plan%20what%20happens%20to,ask%20Google%20to%20delete%20it.
- *The Guide to Getting and Using Your Health Records* https://www.healthit.gov/how-to-get-your-health-record/get-it/
- *FAMILY HISTORY IS IMPORTANT FOR YOUR HEALTH* https://www.ncbi.nlm.nih.gov/books/NBK115560/
- *Quality ID #130: Documentation of Current Medications in the ...* https://qpp.cms.gov/docs/QPP_quality_measure_specifications/CQM-Measures/2023_Measure_130_MIPSCQM.pdf
- *Living wills and advance directives for medical decisions* https://www.mayoclinic.org/healthy-lifestyle/consumer-health/in-depth/living-wills/art-20046303
- *Understanding the Costs of Cremation vs. Burial* https://www.smartcremation.com/articles/understanding-the-costs-of-cremation-vs-burial/
- *13 Different Religious Perspectives on Cremation* https://www.everplans.com/articles/13-different-religious-perspectives-on-cremation
- *How To Personalize a Funeral or Memorial Service*: https://www.funeralwise.com/celebration-of-life/personalize-funeral/
- *How Prepaid Funeral Plans Work: Costs, Expenses, Pros, ...* https://www.lhlic.com/consumer-resources/how-pre-paid-funeral-plans-work/
- *How to Write a Heartfelt Letter: 12 Steps (with Pictures)* https://www.wikihow.com/Write-a-Heartfelt-Letter
- *80 Farewell Messages You Can Use to Say Goodbye* https://www.kudoboard.com/blog/70-farewell-messages-you-can-use-to-say-goodbye/
- *Tips for Recording High-Quality Videos - Teaching at HDS* https://teaching.hds.harvard.edu/tools-for-teaching-2/panopto/tips-for-recording-high-quality-videos/
- *Preserving Your Letters and Documents* https://postalmuseum.si.edu/preserving-your-letters-and-documents
- *How to Set Up a Pet Trust - The Werner Law Firm* https://wernerlawca.com/how-set-up-pet-trust/
- *How to Organize Critical Documents for Emergency ...* https://theprovidentprepper.org/how-to-organize-critical-documents-for-emergency-evacuation/
- *How to Prepare Your Digital Life for Your Death* https://www.pcmag.com/how-to/how-to-prepare-your-digital-life-accounts-for-your-death

- *Using a Personal Property Memorandum With Your Will | Nolo* https://www.nolo.com/legal-encyclopedia/using-personal-property-memorandum-with-your-will.html#:~:text=A%20personal%20property%20memorandum%20allows,and%20destroy%20the%20old%20one.

Made in the USA
Monee, IL
04 November 2026

67377423R00069